Time Series Analysis and Forecasting

The Box–Jenkins approach

Time Series Analysis and Forecasting

The Box–Jenkins approach

O. D. Anderson
B.Sc., M.A., M.Sc., A.F.I.M.A., M.I.S., F.S.S.
*Sometime Senior Lecturer in Statistics and Operational Research,
Department of Computer Science, Lanchester Polytechnic*

Butterworths
London and Boston

THE BUTTERWORTH GROUP

ENGLAND
Butterworth & Co (Publishers) Ltd
London: 88 Kingsway, WC2B 6AB

AUSTRALIA
Butterworths Pty Ltd
Sydney: 586 Pacific Highway, NSW 2067
Melbourne: 343 Little Collins Street, 3000
Brisbane: 240 Queen Street, 4000

CANADA
Butterworth & Co (Canada) Ltd
Toronto: 2265 Midland Avenue, Scarborough, Ontario, M1P 4S1

NEW ZEALAND
Butterworths of New Zealand Ltd
Wellington: 26–28 Waring Taylor Street, 1

SOUTH AFRICA
Butterworth & Co (South Africa) (Pty) Ltd
Durban: 152–154 Gale Street

USA
Butterworth (Publishers) Inc.
161 Ash Street, Reading, Mass. 01867

First published 1975

ISBN 0 408 706759

Text set in 10/11 pt. IBM Press Roman, printed by photolithography,
and bound in Great Britain at The Pitman Press, Bath

Preface

Time Series analysis is concerned with data which are not independent, but serially correlated, and where the relations between consecutive observations are of interest. It is a rapid growth area in statistical practice, and the mass of research and application, currently taking place, is reflected in a flood of papers and conferences.

One of its main applications is to *forecasting,* and the Box–Jenkins approach, developed in the 60s, is attracting more and more attention. There are now very few disciplines in the Sciences, Business and Technology, which are not investigating its possibilities. It is therefore not surprising that time series analysis, in general, and the Box–Jenkins approach, in particular, is being taught on an ever increasing number of undergraduate and postgraduate courses.

At present there is no work on Box–Jenkins methods of reasonable length and price, and this book is intended to fill the need. It is self-contained and suitable for the numerate student or research worker in the mathematical, physical, technological, business or social sciences, with a first course in statistics behind him. It is expected that such a reader will have access to a digital computer, though this is not essential for much of the book.

The Box–Jenkins approach deals only with the *time domain* and *discrete* data (the complementary *frequency domain* is dealt with in Ref. 1), and this book falls into three parts. First the properties of a flexible class of stable linear statistical models, the ARMA class, are discussed. The Box–Jenkins iterative cycle of Identification, Estimation and Verification is then described for these models, and it is shown how such a satisfactorily fitted model can be used in forecasting. This work is extended to cover certain types of unstable model, the ARIMA and seasonal ARIMA classes. Finally, more recent work, much developed at Nottingham under Professor Granger, is surveyed. This includes

v

further points on forecasting, and ways in which the fitted Box–Jenkins models can be 'explained'.

The use of a number of simulated series will no doubt be criticised. However, it is felt that the beginner should first be shown how the methodology applies in situations where the *process* is accurately known, before attempting to deal with real series.

The large number of exercises, both theoretical and applied, should be considered as an integral part of the book. They reinforce and extend the text they follow. The average reader should be able to attempt most and solve some, and the worked solutions are intended to be compared *after* his effort has been made. The good student will find that, in this way, he is himself able to discover much of the 'book work'.

To anyone familiar with the subject area, my debt to Professors Box and Jenkins is evidently immense. I have not cited their original papers in the bibliography, as they have brought these together (*see* Ref. 2). The remaining authors referenced should indicate what I owe to other workers.

This book developed out of final year undergraduate lectures at Lanchester and research at Nottingham, where Time Series is a major interest, and I am grateful to both the Polytechnic and the University for extensive library and computing facilities.

I hope readers will tell me of any errors or ambiguities they find. I also look forward to other reactions, suggestions, comments and criticisms – indeed to all correction, instruction and information which will help clarify or improve a later edition.

Oliver Anderson
(Now with the Civil Service College,
(London)

Contents

1	Introduction	1
2	Autocorrelation	6
3	Box–Jenkins	12
4	Autoregressive Processes	15
5	Moving Average Processes	31
6	Mixed Processes	43
7	Identification	54
8	Estimation	68
9	Verification	75
10	Forecasting	90
11	Integrated Processes	99
12	Seasonal Models	124
13	Forecasting: Further Points	134
14	How the Models Arise	137
15	Realisability	146
16	Autoaggregation	153
17	Postscript	157
	Appendix I – Collection of Time Series	159
	Appendix II – Identification Program	167
	Appendix III – Inequality Proof	173
	References	175
	Index	179

1

Introduction

A *time series* is a set of observations ordered in time (or in any other dimension). We will only consider *discrete* series with observations $z(t_i)$ made at times t_i, $i = 1, \ldots, N$, where N, the *length* of the series, is the total number of observations made. Should the original series be *continuous,* one can still *imbed* a discrete series, by taking readings at discrete times, to obtain a *sampled* series, such as A (*Figure 1.1*). The other way a discrete series can arise is by *accumulating* a variable for a length of time, and B (*Figure 1.1*) is such an *accumulated* series.

Often the time interval, $\tau_i = t_{i+1} - t_i$, between successive observations is naturally constant, or can be arranged so, and we have $\tau_i = \tau$ say, $i = 1, \ldots, N - 1$. The transformation, $t \to 1 + (t-t_1)/\tau$, then takes t_i into i, and the observations can be written as $z_i = z(i)$ at 'times' $i = 1, \ldots, N$. Occasionally the convenient period between observations is not quite constant, for instance the calendar month. This will make little difference in the case of a sampled series, but an adjustment will generally be necessary for an accumulated series[3].

If, from past knowledge, the future behaviour of a time series can be exactly predicted, it is a *deterministic* series and requires no further investigation. Otherwise it is a *statistical* series for which, at best, past knowledge can only indicate the probabilistic structure of future behaviour; it is with such series that we will be concerned. In *Figure 1.1* series C is deterministic, whereas A and B are statistical, as are D, E and F.

A statistical series can be considered as a single realisation of some underlying *statistical* (or *stochastic*) *process*. *Figure 1.2* shows series F together with some other realisations of the same generating process, a sample of series from the population or *ensemble* of series defined by the process. Usually it is impossible to obtain other realisations of a statistical process, i.e. one cannot restart economies or the weather to see what other patterns they might have followed.

1

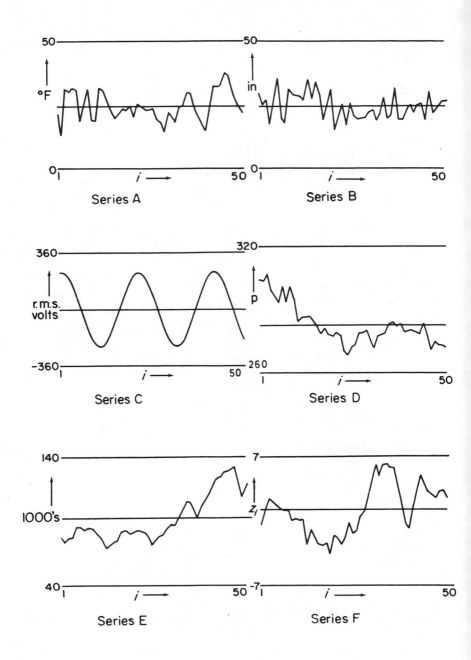

Series A

Series B

Series C

Series D

Series E

Series F

Evidently any z_i is a realisation of some random variable Z_i with an associated p.d.f., probability density function, $p(z_i)$; and any set of Z_i, say $Z_{j_1}, \ldots, Z_{j_r}$, has a joint p.d.f., $p(z_{j_1}, \ldots, z_{j_r})$. If a statistical process is such that $p(z_{i+n_1}, \ldots, z_{i+n_m})$ is independent of i for any positive integer m, and any choice of $n_1, \ldots, n_m$, then the probabilistic structure does not change with time and the process is said to be *strictly*

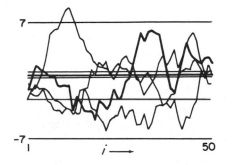

*Figure 1.2   Series F (thick line), with other repeated simulations of its under-
lying process*

stationary. Otherwise it is *non stationary.* If the definition holds, but with the restriction $m \leqslant p$, where p is a positive integer, then there is *stationarity* of *order p.* For a *gaussian* process, which is defined by the property that the p.d.f. associated with any set of times is multivariate normal, strict stationarity requires only stationarity of order 2, since all moments of higher order are necessarily zero. Consequently it is usual to be satisfied with stationarity of order 2, called *weak stationarity,* and to make the hopefully plausible assumption of normality. These terms also apply when 'process' is replaced by 'series'.

Weak stationarity implies that for all i

$$E[Z_i] = \mu$$

Figure 1.1   Examples of time series (of length 50) with mean levels indicated.
Series A: *Daily drybulb temperatures (°F) at noon on Ben Nevis, Feb. 1st –
Mar. 21st 1884*[4]. **Series B:** *Annual rainfall (ins) at Nottingham Castle, 1867 –
1916 (no correction for leap years)*[5]. **Series C:** *AC single phase voltage across
household mains, at intervals of 0·001 s.* **Series D:** *ICI closing stock prices (new
pence), Aug. 25th – Nov. 3rd 1972*[6]. **Series E:** *Women unemployed (1000's) in
UK on 1st of each month, June 1968 – July 1972*[7]. **Series F:** *A simulated series
obtained from relation $z_i = 0·9z_{i-1} + a_i$ with $z_0 = 0$, where the a_i were successive
standardised normal variates from a random number generator*[53]

and

$$\text{Cov}\,[Z_i, Z_{i-k}] = \gamma_k$$

where μ and γ_k, all integers k, are constants. μ is the *mean* of the process, the level about which the Z_i fluctuate, and γ_k is the *autocovariance* at *lag k*. In particular, Z_i has constant variance

$$\sigma_z^2 = \gamma_0$$

Also, for all integers k,

$$\gamma_{-k} = \gamma_k$$

since

$$\text{Cov}\,[Z_i, Z_{i+k}] = \text{Cov}\,[Z_{i+k}, Z_i] = \text{Cov}\,[Z_i, Z_{i-k}]$$

and so it is only necessary to determine γ_k for $k \geqslant 0$. The set $\{\gamma_k : k = 0, 1, \ldots\}$ is called the *autocovariance function*.

The *autocorrelation* at lag k is defined by

$$\rho_k = \frac{\text{Cov}\,[Z_i, Z_{i-k}]}{\left\{\text{Var}\,[Z_i]\,\text{Var}\,[Z_{i-k}]\right\}^{\frac{1}{2}}}$$

so

$$\rho_k = \gamma_k/\gamma_0$$

and is independent of the measurement scale. The *autocorrelation function*, abbreviated to a.c.f., is formed by the set $\{\rho_k : k = 0, 1, \ldots\}$, where evidently $\rho_0 = 1$; and an example of it is given in *Figure 1.3*.

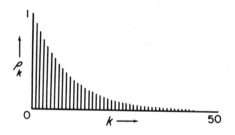

Figure 1.3   Theoretical a.c.f. for the process which generated series F

Unfortunately, for estimating these *ensemble* values, there is often only one realisation of the process available. When the process is stationary and the structure does not change with time, it appears reasonable to average over time instead, obtaining *time* values. In fact, this is sound only if the process is also *ergodic*[8], when the probabilistic structure of all realisations is the same. For instance, if the process were $z_i \equiv c$, where $c \sim N(0, 1)$ is constant for each (hypothetical) realisation, $= 1$ say, for the observed series, then the series mean of 1 does not equal the process mean of 0. The series and the process are stationary, but the process is *not* ergodic. However in practice, when only one realisation exists, it is generally this particular series which is of interest. Thus, nothing is usually lost by forgetting the ensemble, and just considering the series statistics — or those of that sub-ensemble which *is* ergodic with it.

In the literature, little care is taken to distinguish between a random variable and its realisation by means of large and small letters, so we will now drop this convention and allow 'process' or 'series' to be understood from the context.

Almost all the series used in this book are enumerated in Appendix I. Series A to F, excepting C, are listed as the first 50 terms of the longer series A* to F*.

2

Autocorrelation

Given a stationary series $z_1, \ldots, z_N$ one can estimate μ and $\{\gamma_k : k = 0, 1, \ldots\}$ by suitable statistics, which are now usually taken to be

$$\hat{\mu} = \bar{z} = \frac{1}{N} \sum_{1}^{N} z_i$$

and, for $k = 0, 1, \ldots$,

$$\hat{\gamma}_k = c_k = \frac{1}{N} \sum_{k+1}^{N} (z_i - \bar{z})(z_{i-k} - \bar{z}) \tag{2.1}$$

Evidently for any precision in the estimates, N will need to be sufficiently large, and in practice this generally requires $N > 50$ (*see* Reid[9]). Obviously c_k cannot be calculated for $k > N-1$, and again in practice it should not be calculated for $k > N/4$, say. Each ρ_k is then estimated by

$$r_k = c_k/c_0$$

For a stationary normal process, *Bartlett's* formula[10] states that, assuming $\rho_k = 0$ for all $k > K$,

$$\text{Cov}[r_k, r_{k-s}] \simeq \frac{1}{N} \sum_{-K+s}^{K} \rho_i \rho_{i-s} \tag{2.2}$$

This shows that successive values of r_k can be highly correlated, so that

6

the estimated a.c.f. can be very misleading. Putting $s = 0$ in Bartlett's formula gives for all $k > K$

$$\text{Var}\,[r_k] \simeq \frac{1}{N} \sum_{-K}^{K} \rho_i^2 \qquad (2.3)$$

and for fairly large N, if $\rho_k = 0$, r_k is approximately normally distributed[11].

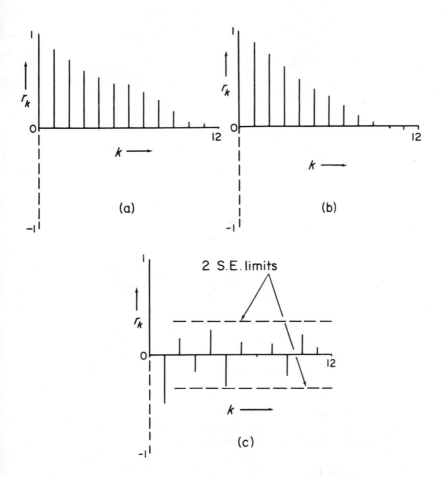

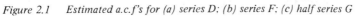

Figure 2.1   Estimated a.c.f's for (a) series D; (b) series F; (c) half series G

In practice, one usually has to replace the ρ_i by r_i in these results. Then equation 2.3 becomes

$$\text{Var}\,[r_k] \; \simeq \; \frac{1}{N}\,(1 + 2 \sum_{1}^{K} r_i^2) \qquad (2.4)$$

and the square root of this is the *large-lag standard error* of r_k.

Exercise 2.1   For series D (Appendix I) (a) calculate r_1 from the first 8 values, and (b) write a program to obtain $r_1, \ldots, r_{12}$ for all 50 values.

Solution: (a) $\bar{z} = 288 + \frac{1}{8}(+1-3+1-2+0-1+0+4) = 288$

$$c_0 = \quad \tfrac{1}{8}(1+9+1+4+0+1+0+16) \; = 4$$

$$c_1 = \quad \tfrac{1}{8}(-3-3-2-0-0-0+0) \; = -1$$

so

$$r_1 = -0\cdot25 \text{ though this is based on far too few values.}$$

(b)

k	1	2	3	4	5	6	7	8	9	10	11	12
r_k	0·84	0·73	0·61	0·54	0·47	0·46	0·38	0·29	0·17	0·05	0·04	−0·01

See Figure 2.1 (a).

Exercise 2.2   Obtain the estimated a.c.f. for series F (Appendix I).

Solution: See *Figure 2.1(b)*. Note the similarity with *Figure 2.1(a)* and how the theoretical pattern of *Figure 1.3* is roughly followed.

Exercise 2.3   Simulate the first 50 terms from the process $z_i = a_i - 0\cdot6\,a_{i-1}$, where the a_i are independent standardised normal variates. Obtain the estimated a.c.f. and consider the hypothesis $\rho_k = 0, k > 1$.

Solution: Figure 2.1(c), shows $r_1, \ldots, r_{12}$ for a typical simulation, listed as the first half of series G (Appendix I). Under the hypothesis of $\rho_k = 0, k > 1$, Bartlett's formula (equation 2.4) gives

$$\text{Var}\,[r_k] \; \simeq \; \frac{1}{N}(1+2r_1^2) = \frac{1}{50}\,\{1+2 \times (-0\cdot507)^2\} = 0\cdot03028$$

so, for $k > 1$,

$$2 \text{ S.E. } [r_k] \simeq 0.348$$

The figure shows that none of $r_2, \ldots, r_{12}$ are significant, so the hypothesis is not rejected.

The *autocorrelation matrix* for a stationary series of length N is given by

$$P_N = \begin{bmatrix} 1 & \rho_1 & \rho_2 & \cdots \rho_{N-1} \\ \rho_1 & 1 & \rho_1 & \rho_{N-2} \\ \rho_2 & \rho_1 & 1 & \rho_{N-3} \\ & & & \\ & \cdot & & \cdot \\ & \cdot & & \cdot \\ & \cdot & & \cdot \\ \rho_{N-1} & \rho_{N-2} & \rho_{N-3} \cdots & 1 \end{bmatrix}$$

which is positive definite. For consider any choice of constants $\lambda_1, \ldots, \lambda_N$, not all zero, and $v = \lambda_1 z_1 + \ldots + \lambda_N z_N = \boldsymbol{\lambda}^I z$. Then Var $[v]$, which is necessarily positive, $= \boldsymbol{\lambda}^T P_N \boldsymbol{\lambda} \sigma_z^2$. So $\boldsymbol{\lambda}^T P_N \boldsymbol{\lambda}$ is positive for all non-trivial $\boldsymbol{\lambda}$, which implies that P_N is positive definite.

In consequence the a.c.f., and so also the autocovariance function, suffer many constraints. For instance,

$$\begin{vmatrix} 1 & \rho_1 & \rho_2 \\ \rho_1 & 1 & \rho_1 \\ \rho_2 & \rho_1 & 1 \end{vmatrix} > 0 \Rightarrow (1 - \rho_2)(1 + \rho_2 - 2\rho_1^2) > 0$$

and since $1 > \rho_2$, this gives

$$\rho_2 > 2\rho_1^2 - 1$$

It is in part to satisfy these constraints that, in the formula for c_k, the divisor N is used rather than $N-k$, which would yield an unbiased estimate. The mean square errors, m.s.e's, of the estimators are also usually smaller when using N (*see* Jenkins and Watts[12]).

Another tool, which will be needed is the *partial autocorrelation function*, p.a.c.f., denoted by $\{\phi_{kk}: k = 1, 2, \ldots\}$, the set of *partial autocorrelations* at various lags k. These are defined by

$$\phi_{kk} = |P_k^*| / |P_k|$$

where P_k is the $k \times k$ autocorrelation matrix, and P_k^* is P_k with the last column replaced by

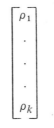

So

$$\phi_{11} = \rho_1$$

$$\phi_{22} = \begin{vmatrix} 1 & \rho_1 \\ \rho_1 & \rho_2 \end{vmatrix} \Bigg/ \begin{vmatrix} 1 & \rho_1 \\ \rho_1 & 1 \end{vmatrix}$$

$$= \frac{\rho_2 - \rho_1^2}{1 - \rho_2^2}$$

etc., and estimates $\hat{\phi}_{kk}$ can be obtained by replacing the ρ_i by r_i.

At lags large enough for the p.a.c.f. to have died out, *Quenouille's* formula[13] gives

$$\text{Var } [\hat{\phi}_{kk}] \simeq \frac{1}{N}$$

so

$$\text{S.E. } [\hat{\phi}_{kk}] \simeq \frac{1}{\sqrt{N}}$$

and again, for fairly large N, $\hat{\phi}_{kk}$ is approximately normally distributed. An example is shown in *Figure 2.2*.

Exercise 2.4 For series D (Appendix I), calculate $\hat{\phi}_{11}, \hat{\phi}_{22}, \hat{\phi}_{33}$, and then consider the hypothesis $\phi_{kk} = 0, k > 1$.

Solution: Using the results from exercise 2.1

$$\hat{\phi}_{11} = 0.84$$

$$\hat{\phi}_{22} = \frac{0.73 - 0.84^2}{1 - 0.84^2} = 0.08$$

$$\hat{\phi}_{33} = \begin{vmatrix} 1 & 0\cdot84 & 0\cdot84 \\ 0\cdot84 & 1 & 0\cdot73 \\ 0\cdot73 & 0\cdot84 & 0\cdot61 \end{vmatrix} \bigg/ \begin{vmatrix} 1 & 0\cdot84 & 0\cdot73 \\ 0\cdot84 & 1 & 0\cdot84 \\ 0\cdot73 & 0\cdot84 & 1 \end{vmatrix} = \frac{0\cdot006476}{0\cdot086076} = -0\cdot075$$

Under the hypothesis of $\phi_{kk} = 0$, $k = 1,2,...,$ Quenouille's formula gives, for $k > 1$,

$$\text{Var}\,[\hat{\phi}_{kk}] \simeq 1/50$$

so

$$2\,\text{S.E.}\,[\hat{\phi}_{kk}] \simeq 0\cdot28$$

Thus $\hat{\phi}_{22}$ and $\hat{\phi}_{33}$ are not significant, and these (meagre) calculations show no evidence for rejecting the hypothesis. Note again the similarity with the theoretical p.a.c.f. of series F in *Figure 2.2.*

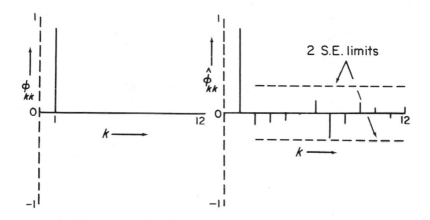

Figure 2.2   Theoretical and estimated p.a.c.f's for series F

3

Box-Jenkins

The *Box–Jenkins* method[2] for analysing time series uses the *backshift operator, B*, defined by

$$Bz_i = z_{i-1}$$

and the *difference operator,* ∇, defined by

$$\nabla z_i = z_i - z_{i-1}$$

These two operators are evidently connected by the relation

$$\nabla = 1 - B$$

and obey the laws of elementary algebra.

Models of statistical processes of the form

$$\phi(B)z_i = \theta(B)a_i \tag{3.1}$$

are frequently used, where ϕ and θ are polynomials, and $\{a_i\}$ is a series of *shocks* generated by a *white noise* process, for which the a_i are independently and normally distributed with zero mean and constant variance, σ_a^2. This can be conveniently summarised as $a_i \sim IN(0, \sigma_a^2)$. For all the simulations in this book σ_a^2 is intended to be unity, and *Figure 3.1* shows an example of such a white noise series, together with its estimated a.c.f. and p.a.c.f.

Exercise 3.1 Check that the 2 S.E. limit lines in *Figure 3.1* are correctly given.

Solution: $z_i \sim IN(0,1)$, so $\mu = 0$ and $\rho_k = 0, k > 1$. Thus, for $k > 1$, Bartlett's formula gives S.E. $[r_k] = 1/\sqrt{64}$, and since $\phi_{kk} \equiv 0/1$, S.E. $[\hat{\phi}_{kk}] = 1/\sqrt{64}$ also.

Therefore the 2 S.E. limit lines for both estimated functions are ±0·25 from the axes as shown, and none of the r_k or $\hat{\phi}_{kk}$ are significant.

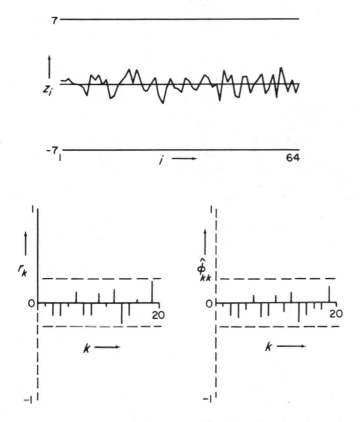

Figure 3.1   White noise simulation $z_i = a_i$ with estimated a.c.f. and p.a.c.f.

Rewriting equation 3.1 as

$$z_i = \psi(B)a_i \qquad (3.2)$$

where $\psi(B) = \theta(B)/\phi(B)$, we can consider $\{z_i\}$ to be generated by passing the white noise process $\{a_i\}$ through a *linear filter* with *transfer function* $\psi(B)$.

When dealing with functions, such as $\alpha(B) = \alpha_0 + \alpha_1 B + \alpha_2 B^2 + \ldots$, the α_j are referred to as the *weights* of the function. The reason for this is seen by considering equation 3.2, in which z_i can be considered as a weighted sum of the current and previous shocks.

An example of equation 3.1 is the model

$$z_i = \phi\, z_{i-1} + a_i, a_i \sim IN(0,\sigma_a^2)$$

and its probabilistic behaviour is easily determined for given ϕ and σ_a^2 (*see* Chapter 4). Putting $\phi = 0\cdot9$ and $\sigma_a^2 = 1$ gives the generator for series F (*Figure 1.1*).

The Box–Jenkins method hopes, from inspection of the estimated a.c.f. and p.a.c.f., obtained from an observed time series, to recognise patterns which could be explained by some such model. After this *identification*, it proceeds to efficiently estimate the values of the various parameters, the *estimation* stage, and then performs *verification* tests to determine whether the 'fitted' model is adequate. If it is not, these very tests should indicate how the model ought to be modified, and a further cycle of identification, estimation and verification is instigated.

Evidently several candidates might be suggested at the identification stage, and, if fully investigated, distinct models might show up as adequate. To reduce these, the usual statistical principle of *parsimony* is employed, where models prodigal in parameters are neglected in favour of those which are economical.

We will spend the next three chapters investigating the properties of various groups of models comprising the ARMA class, which experience shows are frequently useful in explaining stationary series that occur in practice. We will then, in Chapters 7, 8 and 9, look at the three stages of the Box–Jenkins method. In Chapter 10 it will be shown how the fitted models can be used in forecasting, and then in 11 and 12 we will extend our ideas to certain types of non-stationary process. Chapter 11 is concerned with removing non-stationarity by *differencing*, and Chapter 12 deals with *seasonal* series — the major contribution made by Professors Box and Jenkins.

4

Autoregressive Processes

The general form for an *autoregressive process* of order p, an AR(p) process, is

$$z_i = \phi_1 z_{i-1} + \ldots + \phi_p z_{i-p} + a_i \qquad (4.1)$$

where the current value of the process is expressed as a weighted sum of past values plus the current shock. Thus z_i can be considered to be *regressed* on the p previous z's, hence the name. We can rewrite equation 4.1 as

$$\phi(B) z_i = a_i \qquad (4.2)$$

where $\phi(B) = 1 - \phi_1 B - \ldots - \phi_p B^p$ is termed the AR(p) *operator.*

Consider the AR(1) process with model

$$z_i = \phi z_{i-1} + a_i \qquad (4.3)$$

where as usual the random shocks $a_i \sim IN(0, \sigma_a^2)$, and the model is assumed stationary. Since a_i is independent of z_{i-1}, taking variances gives

$$\sigma_z^2 = \phi^2 \sigma_z^2 + \sigma_a^2$$

so

$$\sigma_z^2 (1 - \phi^2) = \sigma_a^2$$

and, for σ_z^2 to be finite and non-negative, this requires

$$-1 < \phi < 1$$

This is the condition for stationarity. It could be written as '$1 - \phi B$ has its zero of magnitude > 1', and in general the *necessary and sufficient condition for an* AR(p) *process to be stationary is that the zeros of $\phi(B)$ should all lie outside the unit circle.*

15

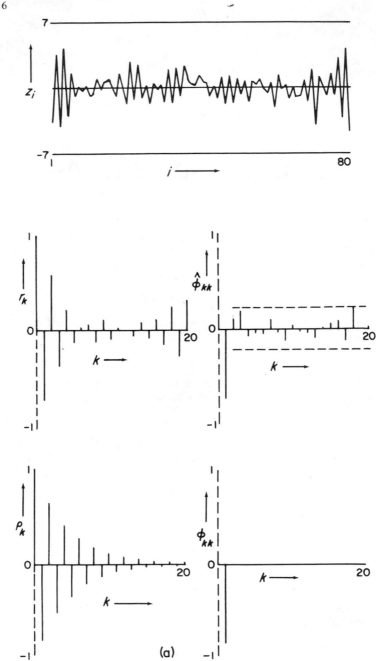

(a)

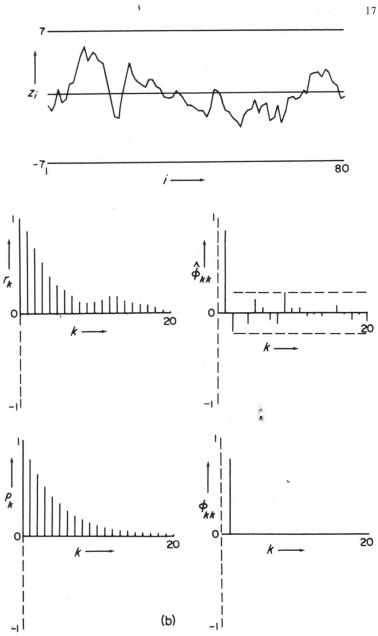

Figure 4.1   Simulated AR(1) processes (of length 80)
            (a) $z_i = -0.8z_{i-1} + a_i$;   (b) $z_i = 0.8z_{i-1} + a_i$

Taking expectations in equation 4.3

$$\mu = \phi\mu + 0$$

so, since $\phi \neq 1$,

$$\mu = 0$$

Multiplying through by z_{i-k} in equation 4.3, and taking expectations

$$E\left[z_i\, z_{i-k}\right] = \phi E\left[z_{i-1}\, z_{i-k}\right] + E\left[a_i\, z_{i-k}\right]$$

So for $k \geqslant 1$, which ensures that a_i and z_{i-k} are independent,

$$\gamma_k = \phi\gamma_{k-1}$$

a first-order difference equation with solution

$$\gamma_k = \phi^k\gamma_0$$

or

$$\rho_k = \phi^k, \; k \geqslant 1$$

Figure 4.1 shows realisations of AR(1) processes together with their theoretical and estimated a.c.f's. For $\phi = 0.8$, a large positive value, adjacent terms of the series are highly correlated and the a.c.f's follow slow geometric decays. However, for the negative ϕ, the a.c.f's alternate in sign as they decay to zero. In particular, ρ_1 has a large negative value, adjacent terms of the series have a high negative correlation and the 'low-frequency' trends of series (b) are replaced by violent rapid oscillation in series (a).

The theoretical p.ac.f. is given by a single term

$$\phi_{11} = \rho_1 = \phi$$

since

$$\phi_{kk} = 0, k > 1$$

For instance,

$$\phi_{22} = \frac{\rho_2 - \rho_1^2}{1 - \rho_1^2} = \frac{\phi^2 - \phi^2}{1 - \phi^2} = 0, \text{ since } \phi^2 \neq 1$$

For rather short series, such as those of *Figure 4.1,* the estimated functions (whatever the process) will only roughly follow the theoretical patterns. There will always be minor discrepancies, and occasionally there will be *chance* significant ones. Equation 2.2 shows that successive r_k (and so $\hat{\phi}_{kk}$) are not uncorrelated, and consequently for a set of 20 r_k, say, we would not expect about one to be significant at the 5% level. It is more likely that usually none will be significant, though sometimes several will be. However, for 20 assorted simulations, even if the random number generator employed were 'perfect', one *would* expect more than one r_k (or $\hat{\phi}_{kk}$) sequence to be significant. In fact several of the simulations in this book prove to be *chance* significant, but this is an underestimate since some of these are resimulations, the first attempts giving 'untypical' a.c.f s. In *Figure 4.1(a)* the estimated a.c.f. builds up at higher lags, a not infrequent occurrence.

Exercise 4.1   Use Bartlett's formula (equation 2.4) to obtain $\lim_{k \to \infty}$ Var $[r_k]$ for an AR(1) process.

Solution:

$$\lim_{k \to \infty} \text{Var} [r_k] \simeq \frac{1}{N} \left(1 + 2 \sum_{i=1}^{\infty} \phi^{2i}\right) = \frac{1}{N} \left(\frac{1 + \phi^2}{1 - \phi^2}\right)$$

Exercise 4.2   Find the region of stationarity, mean, variance, a.c.f. and p.a.c.f. for the AR (2) process

$$z_i = \phi_1 z_{i-1} + \phi_2 z_{i-2} + a_i \tag{4.4}$$

Solution: Taking expectations

$$\mu = \phi_1 \mu + \phi_2 \mu$$

which requires $\mu = 0$, for stationarity, since $\phi(1) \neq 0$. So multiplying through equation 4.4 by z_{i-k} and taking expectations, for $k = 0$,

$$\sigma_z^2 = \phi_1 \gamma_1 + \phi_2 \gamma_2 + \sigma_a^2$$

or

$$\sigma_z^2 (1 - \phi_1 \rho_1 - \phi_2 \rho_2) = \sigma_a^2 \tag{4.5}$$

since the only part of z_i correlated with a_i is the most recent shock a_i; and for $k \geq 1$,

$$\gamma_k = \phi_1 \gamma_{k-1} + \phi_2 \gamma_{k-2}$$

or

$$\rho_k = \phi_1 \rho_{k-1} + \phi_2 \rho_{k-2} \tag{4.6}$$

a second-order difference equation which can be easily solved.

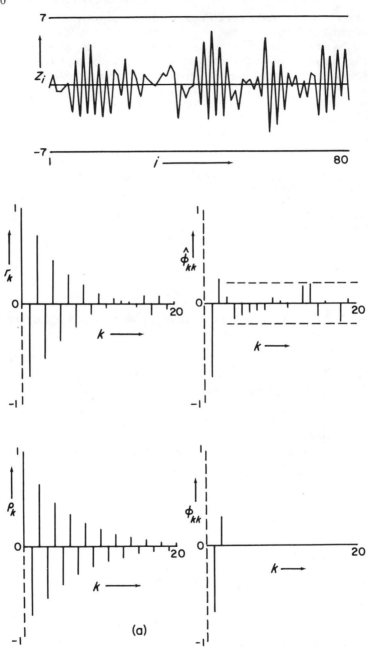

(a)

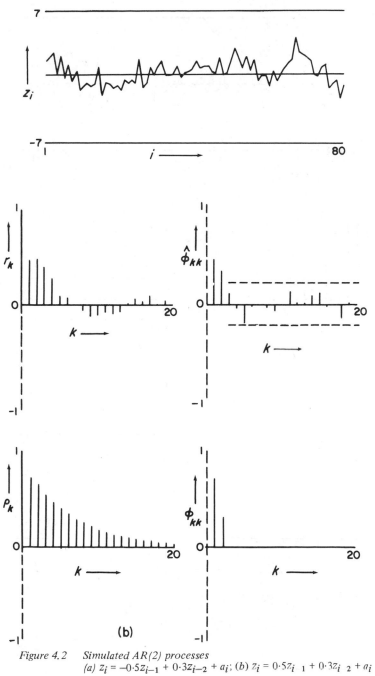

Figure 4.2   Simulated AR(2) processes
(a) $z_i = -0.5z_{i-1} + 0.3z_{i-2} + a_i$; (b) $z_i = 0.5z_{i-1} + 0.3z_{i-2} + a_i$
((c) and (d) overleaf)

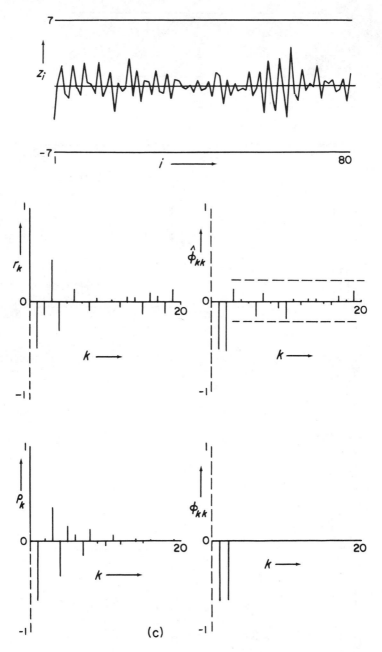

(c)

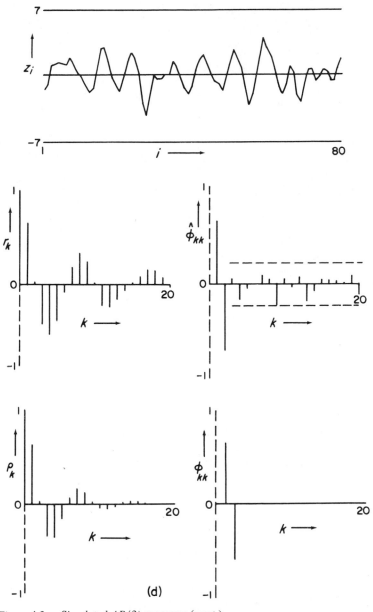

Figure 4.2   Simulated AR(2) processes (cont.)
(c) $z_i = -z_{i-1} - 0.6z_{i-2} + a_i$; (d) $z_i = z_{i-1} - 0.6z_{i-2} + a_i$

However, in practice, it is simpler to start with

$$\rho_0 = 1 \qquad (4.7)$$

$$\rho_1 = \phi_1 + \phi_2 \rho_{-1} \Rightarrow \rho_1 = \frac{\phi_1}{1-\phi_2} \qquad (4.8)$$

and then use equation 4.6 as a recurrence relation to obtain ρ_k, $k \geqslant 2$. In particular

$$\rho_2 = \frac{\phi_1^2}{1-\phi_2} + \phi_2$$

so equation 4.5 gives

$$\sigma_z^2 \left[1 - \frac{\phi_1^2}{1-\phi_2} - \phi_2 \left(\frac{\phi_1^2}{1-\phi_2} + \phi_2 \right) \right] = \sigma_a^2$$

or

$$\sigma_z^2 = \frac{(1-\phi_2)\sigma_a^2}{(1+\phi_2)(1-\phi_1-\phi_2)(1+\phi_1-\phi_2)}$$

For each factor in the denominator to be positive, necessarily

$$\left. \begin{array}{c} -1 < \phi_2 \\ \phi_1 + \phi_2 < 1 \\ -\phi_1 + \phi_2 < 1 \end{array} \right\} \qquad (4.9)$$

which gives the region of stationarity. It follows that

$$\phi_2 < 1 \qquad (4.9a)$$

Finally

$$\phi_{11} = \rho_1 = \frac{\phi_1}{1-\phi_2}$$

$$\phi_{22} = \frac{\rho_2 - \rho_1^2}{1 - \rho_1^2} = \phi_2$$

and, for $k > 2$,

$$\phi_{kk} = 0$$

so the p.a.c.f. has just two terms.

Examples of AR(2) processes are shown in *Figure 4.2*. Note now that four basic patterns can exist for the ρ_k , all decaying to zero. Denoting the left and right members of each cair of series by L and R, respectively, we see that

$$L\rho_k = (-1)^k \; R\rho_k$$

and

$$L\phi_{kk} = (-1)^k \; R\phi_{kk}$$

as was also the case for the AR(1) pair of series in *Figure 4.1*.

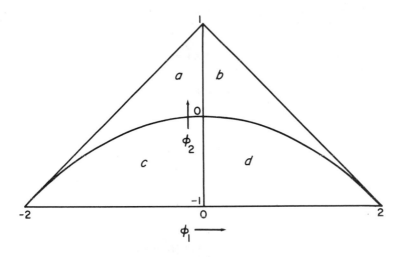

Figure 4.3   *Triangular stationarity region for AR(2) processes*

The four patterns correspond to the four regions in *Figure 4.3*, which constitute the triangle of stationarity, defined by the inequalities 4.9. In regions (c) and (d), the zeros of $\phi(B)$ are complex, and this gives rise to pseudo-periodic behaviour in (d), as exemplified by the series plot and the a.c.f's.

It would appear that in practice rather short realisations of processes, such as (a) and (b), might well be initially identified as AR(1), owing to ϕ_{22} (fixed) not being much larger than $2/\sqrt{80}$. This will become less likely as N increases. The wavelike $\{r_k\}$ of (b) is a not uncommon *chance* modification of a basic $\{\rho_k\}$ pattern. Finally, note that three of the realisations have a later $\hat{\phi}_{kk}$ about significant at the 5% level.

It is generally true that, if one knows the process, one can recognise the theoretical patterns in the estimated functions. But if one does not, it is not so easy to infer the theoretical pattern (and hence the process). This is so when dealing with simulated series, and the problem of *identifying* a real process, which will not even follow any idealised model exactly, is thus considerable.

Exercise 4.3   Solve the difference equation 4.6.

Solution: Try $\rho_k = \lambda^k$, then

$$\lambda^2 - \phi_1 \lambda - \phi_2 = 0 \tag{4.10}$$

So $1/\lambda$ satisfies $\phi(B) = 0$, and the general solution is

$$\rho_k = A_1 \lambda_1^k + A_2 \lambda_2^k$$

where $1/\lambda_1$, $1/\lambda_2$ are the zeros of $\phi(B)$, and A_1, A_2 are constants to be determined. From equation 4.7,

$$A_1 + A_2 = 1$$

and, using equation 4.10, equation 4.8 gives

$$A_1 \lambda_1 + A_2 \lambda_2 = \frac{\lambda_1 + \lambda_2}{1 + \lambda_1 \lambda_2}$$

These yield

$$A_1 = \frac{\lambda_1 (1 - \lambda_2^2)}{(\lambda_1 - \lambda_2)(1 + \lambda_1 \lambda_2)}$$

$$A_2 = \frac{-\lambda_2 (1 - \lambda_1^2)}{(\lambda_1 - \lambda_2)(1 + \lambda_1 \lambda_2)}$$

For the general AR(p) process, $E[z_i]$ is again zero and the recurrence relation for the ρ_k is easily obtained as

$$\rho_k = \phi_1 \rho_{k-1} + \ldots + \phi_p \rho_{k-p}, k > 0 \tag{4.11}$$

The starting values $\rho_0, \ldots, \rho_{p-1}$ are obtained as for the second-order process, and thence the ρ_k for $k \gg p$. The stationarity conditions will be complicated; however, assuming that they are obeyed, the variance is obtained in the same way and is given by

$$\sigma_z^2 (1 - \phi_1 \rho_1 - \ldots - \phi_p \rho_p) = \sigma_a^2 \tag{4.12}$$

The p.a.c.f. will now have p terms, as is shown on p. 28.

    An interesting alternative form for equation 4.11 is

$$\phi(B) \rho_k = 0, k > 0 \tag{4.13}$$

where B is now considered to operate on k. This could have been derived as follows. Multiplying equation 4.2 by z_{i-k} gives

$$z_{i-k} \, (\phi \, (B) \, z_i) = z_{i-k} \, a_i$$

and taking expectations for $k > 0$ yields equation 4.13.

Writing out equation 4.11 for $k = 1, \ldots, p$ we obtain the *Yule–Walker* equations, which can be combined in matrix form as

$$
\begin{bmatrix} \rho_1 \\ \cdot \\ \cdot \\ \cdot \\ \cdot \\ \rho_p \end{bmatrix}
=
\begin{bmatrix}
1 & \rho_1 & \cdot & \cdot & \cdot & \rho_{p-1} \\
\rho_1 & 1 & & & & \rho_{p-2} \\
\cdot & & \cdot & & & \cdot \\
\cdot & & & \cdot & & \cdot \\
\cdot & & & & \cdot & \cdot \\
\rho_{p-1} & \rho_{p-2} & \cdot & \cdot & \cdot & 1
\end{bmatrix}
\begin{bmatrix} \phi_1 \\ \cdot \\ \cdot \\ \cdot \\ \cdot \\ \phi_p \end{bmatrix}
$$

or briefly

$$\boldsymbol{\rho} = P_p \, \boldsymbol{\phi}$$

This has the solution

$$\boldsymbol{\phi} = P_p^{-1} \, \boldsymbol{\rho} \qquad (4.14)$$

so for an AR(p) model, given the ρ's we can find the ϕ's.

For example, for AR(1)

$$\phi_1 = \rho_1$$

and for AR(2)

$$
\begin{bmatrix} \phi_1 \\ \phi_2 \end{bmatrix}
=
\dfrac{\begin{bmatrix} 1 & -\rho_1 \\ -\rho_1 & 1 \end{bmatrix} \begin{bmatrix} \rho_1 \\ \rho_2 \end{bmatrix}}{1 - \rho_1^2}
$$

so

$$\phi_1 = \rho_1 \, (1-\rho_2)/(1-\rho_1^2)$$

$$\phi_2 = (\rho_2-\rho_1^2)/(1-\rho_1^2)$$

Replacing the ρ_k by r_k, we obtain the *Yule–Walker estimates* for the autoregressive parameters.

For an AR(k) model, denoting the matrix of cofactors of P_k by $[\pi_{ij}]$, equation 4.14 gives

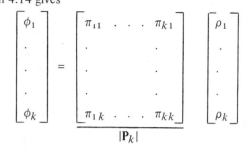

So

$$\phi_k = \frac{\displaystyle\sum_{i=1}^{k} \pi_{ik}\rho_i}{|P_k|} = \frac{|P_k^*|}{|P_k|} = \phi_{kk}$$

the partial autocorrelation at lag k. Thus for an AR(p) process, ϕ_{kk} is zero for $k > p$, since we can consider the model to be AR(k) with $\phi_{p+1} = \ldots = \phi_k = 0$, and the p.a.c.f. cuts off after p terms. Further, for any process, the estimated p.a.c.f. can be considered as the set of final parameters obtained when successive AR(k) models, $k = 1, \ldots$, are fitted to the data.

Exercise 4.4   For an AR(p) process show that a necessary condition for stationarity is that all the zeros of $\phi\,(B)$ lie outside the unit circle.

Solution:

$$z_i = \phi^{-1}\,(B)\,a_i = \left[\prod_{r=1}^{p} (1-\lambda_r B) \right]^{-1} a_i$$

where $1/\lambda_r, r = 1, \ldots, p$, are the zeros of $\phi(B)$. Expressing this in partial fractions, if the λ_r are all distinct, there exist l_r such that

$$z_i = \left[\sum_{r=1}^{p} \frac{l_r}{(1-\lambda_r B)} \right] a_i$$

Then

$$z_i = \sum_{r=1}^{p} \left(l_r \sum_{k=0}^{\infty} \lambda_r{}^k a_{i-k} \right)$$

$$= \sum_{k=0}^{\infty} \left(\sum_{r=1}^{p} l_r \lambda_r{}^k \right) a_{i-k}$$

and

$$\sigma_z^2 = \sum_{k=0}^{\infty} \left(\sum_{r=1}^{p} l_r \lambda_r{}^k \right)^2 \sigma_a^2$$

Now, for stationarity, necessarily σ_z^2 is finite, so $|\lambda_r| < 1, r = 1, \ldots, p$; that is, the zeros of $\phi(B)$ must all lie outside the unit circle.

This argument can be extended to the cases where the zeros of $\phi(B)$ are not all distinct. For instance, if $\lambda_{p-1} = \lambda_p$, there exist l_r^* such that

$$z_i = \left(\sum_{r=1}^{p-1} \frac{l_r^*}{(1-\lambda_r B)} + \frac{l_p^*}{(1-\lambda_p B)} \right) a_i$$

so

$$\sigma_z^2 = \sum_{k=0}^{\infty} \left(\sum_{r=1}^{p-1} l_r^* \lambda_r{}^k + l_p^*(k+1) \lambda_p{}^k \right)^2 \sigma_a^2$$

and the same condition is still necessary.

Exercise 4.5 Investigate the form of the solution for the difference equation 4.11 when the zeros of $\phi(B)$, $1/\lambda_1, \ldots, 1/\lambda_p$, are distinct and lie outside the unit circle.

Solution: $\phi(B)\rho_k = 0 \Rightarrow \rho_k = \sum_{r=1}^{p} A_r \lambda_r{}^k$, where $A_1, \ldots, A_p$ are

constants obtained by substituting into $\rho_0 = 1$ and equation 4.11, for $k = 1, \ldots, p-1$, and solving simultaneously (cf. solution 4.3).

We have all $|\lambda_r| < 1$, and two possibilities can occur:

1. Some λ_r real $\Rightarrow A_r \lambda_r^k$ decays geometrically, with or without alternate changes in sign.
2. Some pair λ_s, λ_t are complex conjugates with modulus λ, say. Since ρ_k must be real for all k, it follows that $A_s A_t$, are also complex conjugates and

$$A_s \lambda_s^k + A_t \lambda_t^k = A\lambda^k \sin(\omega k + \Omega)$$

where ω and Ω are constants, and the contribution follows a geometrically damped sine wave.

Thus, we see that the solution consists of a sum of geometric decays and decaying sine waves (cf. *Figure 4.2*, for $p = 2$).

Exercise 4.6   Find the a.c.f. for the process $z_i = z_{i-1} - 0 \cdot 25\, z_{i-2} + a_i$.

Solution: $\phi(B) = (1 - 0 \cdot 5B)^2$, so the zeros lie outside the unit circle and the process is stationary. The zeros are coincident and the solution to equation 4.6 is this time

$$\rho_k = (A + Ck)\, 0 \cdot 5^k$$

where $A = 1$ from equation 4.7 and then, using equation 4.8, $C = 0 \cdot 6$.

5

Moving Average Processes

The *moving average model*[†] of order q, the MA(q) process, is given by

$$z_i = a_i + \theta_1 a_{i-1} + \ldots + \theta_q a_{i-q}$$

where, as usual, the $a_i \sim IN(0, \sigma_a^2)$. This can be written

$$z_i = \theta(B)a_i \tag{5.1}$$

where $\theta(B) = 1 + \theta_1 B + \ldots + \theta_q B^q$ is the MA(q) *operator*. Taking variances

$$\sigma_z^2 = (1 + \theta_1^2 + \ldots + \theta_q^2) \sigma_a^2 \tag{5.2}$$

and for finite q, the process is evidently always stationary.

Equation 5.1 can also be written

$$\theta^{-1}(B) z_i = a_i$$

which is of the form

$$z_i - \pi_1 z_{i-1} - \pi_2 z_{i-2} - \ldots = a_i$$

or

$$\pi(B) z_i = a_i \tag{5.3}$$

The MA(q) process is said to be *invertible* if the π weights form a convergent series, i.e. if and only if the zeros of $\theta(B)$ all lie outside the unit circle, a condition analogous to that for stationarity of an AR(p)

[†]'Moving Average' is a somewhat misleading term, as the weights do not generally sum to unity.

process. We will stipulate that all processes considered shall be invertible as well as stationary. As will be seen later, this avoids certain model multiplicities.

Equation 5.3 shows that an MA(q) process is equivalent to an AR process, $\phi(B)z_i = a_i$, with $\phi(B) = \pi(B) = \theta^{-1}(B)$, that is, an AR process of infinite order. In the same way, an AR(p) process, $\phi(B)z_i = a_i$ (which is always invertible), can be written as an MA (∞) process, $z_i = \psi(B)a_i$, where $\psi(B) = \phi^{-1}(B)$.

Thus, autoregressive and moving average processes are to some extent equivalent, and it is to be expected that whenever a low-order model of one type adequately explains a series, so should a high-order model of the other. The principle of parsimony however prompts one to choose the former, even if the essential equivalence of the two had not been realised.

We will now consider the MA(1) process

$$z_i = a_i + \theta \, a_{i-1}$$

where $\{a_i\}$ is a white noise process. For invertibility $-1 < \theta < 1$. Taking expectations $\mu = 0$. Also, for all k,

$$E\left[z_i z_{i-k}\right] = E\left[(a_i + \theta a_{i-1})(a_{i-k} + \theta a_{i-1-k})\right]$$

so

$$\sigma_z^2 = \gamma_0 = (1 + \theta^2) \sigma_a^2$$

$$\gamma_1 = \theta \, \sigma_a^2$$

and

$$\gamma_k = 0, k > 1$$

So the a.c.f. is given by

$$\rho_1 = \frac{\theta}{1 + \theta^2} \tag{5.4}$$

$$\rho_k = 0, k > 1$$

The a.c.f. thus *cuts off* after lag 1 (cf. exercise 2.3). However, the p.a.c.f. experiences no cut-off, though it can be shown to decay geometrically to zero.

Proof: Writing $\rho_1 = \rho$,

$$|P_k{}^*| = \begin{vmatrix} 1 & \rho & & & & & & \rho \\ \rho & 1 & \rho & & & \bigcirc & & 0 \\ & \rho & 1 & \rho & & & & \cdot \\ & & \cdot & \cdot & \cdot & & & \cdot \\ & & & \cdot & \cdot & \cdot & & \cdot \\ & & & & \cdot & \cdot & \cdot & \cdot \\ & & \bigcirc & & & \rho & 1 & \rho & \cdot \\ & & & & & & \rho & 1 & \cdot \\ & & & & & & & \rho & 0 \end{vmatrix}$$

expanding by last column

$$= (-1)^{k-1}\rho \begin{vmatrix} \rho & 1 & \rho & & & & \\ & \rho & 1 & \rho & & \bigcirc & \\ & & \cdot & \cdot & \cdot & & \\ & & & \cdot & \cdot & \cdot & \\ & & & & \cdot & \cdot & \cdot \\ & & \bigcirc & & & \rho & 1 & \rho \\ & & & & & & \rho & 1 \\ & & & & & & & \rho \end{vmatrix}$$

and by repeated expansion by first column $= (-1)^{k-1}\rho^k$

$$= (-1)^{k-1}\theta^k/(1+\theta^2)^k.$$

$$|P_k| = \begin{vmatrix} 1 & \rho & & & & & \\ \rho & 1 & \rho & & & \bigcirc & \\ & \rho & 1 & \rho & & & \\ & & \cdot & \cdot & \cdot & & \\ & & & \cdot & \cdot & \cdot & \\ & & & & \cdot & \cdot & \cdot \\ & & \bigcirc & & & \rho & 1 & \rho \\ & & & & & & \rho & 1 & \rho \\ & & & & & & & \rho & 1 \end{vmatrix}$$

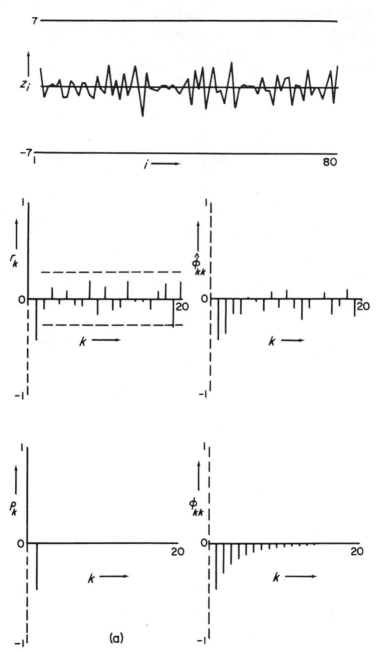

(a)

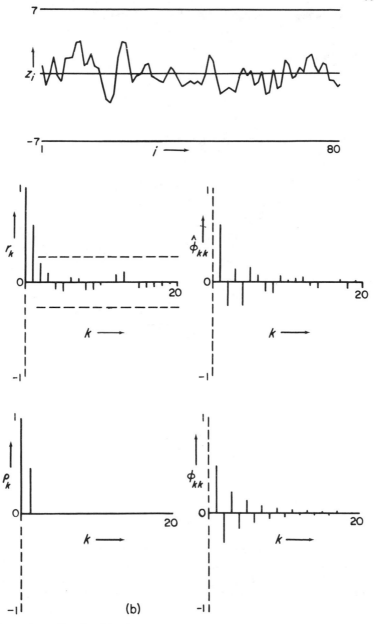

Figure 5.1   *Simulated MA(1) processes*
        (a) $z_i = a_i - 0{\cdot}8a_{i-1}$; *(b)* $z_i = a_i + 0{\cdot}8a_{i-1}$

and expanding by first column and then by first row

$$= |P_{k-1}| - \rho^2 \, |P_{k-2}|$$

Try $|P_k| = \alpha^k$, then

$$\alpha^2 - \alpha + \rho^2 = 0$$

So

$$\alpha = \frac{1 \pm \sqrt{(1 - 4\rho^2)}}{2} = \frac{1}{1 + \theta^2} \text{ or } \frac{\theta^2}{1 + \theta^2}$$

Thus

$$|P_k| = \frac{A + C\theta^{2k}}{(1 + \theta^2)^k}$$

where

$$|P_1| = 1 = \frac{A + C\theta^2}{1 + \theta^2}$$

and

$$|P_2| = 1 - \rho^2 = \frac{1 + \theta^2 + \theta^4}{(1 + \theta^2)^2} = \frac{A + C\theta^4}{(1 + \theta^2)^2}$$

So

$$A = \frac{1}{(1 - \theta^2)} , \quad C = \frac{-\theta^2}{(1 - \theta^2)}$$

and

$$\theta_{kk} = \frac{|P_k^*|}{|P_k|} = \frac{(-1)^{k-1} \, \theta^k \, (1 - \theta^2)}{1 - \theta^{2(k+1)}}$$

Apparently equation 5.4 implies that, corresponding to any ρ_1, there exist in general two possible θ, θ_1 and θ_2 say, and so two possible MA(1) processes. However, from equation 5.4, $\theta_1 \theta_2 = 1$, so this model multiplicity is avoided by stipulating invertibility†.

  Figure 5.1 gives examples of MA(1) processes. For (a) r_{19} is chance significant. Again there is the same relation between the left and right functions, as in Chapter 4, and this will be so in *Figure 5.2* as well.

---

† There does not seem to be much objection to permitting marginal non-invertibility with $\theta_1 = \theta_2 = \pm 1$.

Exercise 5.1   Find the region of invertibility for an MA(2) process, together with its mean, variance and a.c.f.

Solution: The model is of the form

$$z_i = a_i + \theta_1 a_{i-1} + \theta_2 a_{i-2}$$

where $\{a_i\}$ is a white noise process. So

$$E[z_i] = 0$$

For invertibility, by analogy with the stationarity conditions for the AR(2) process,

$$-1 < \theta_2$$
$$-\theta_1 - \theta_2 < 1$$
$$\theta_1 - \theta_2 < 1$$

For all k,

$$E[z_i z_{i-k}] = E[(a_i + \theta_1 a_{i-1} + \theta_2 a_{i-2})(a_{i-k} + \theta_1 a_{i-1-k} + \theta_2 a_{i-2-k})]$$

so

$$\sigma_z^2 = \gamma_0 = (1 + \theta_1^2 + \theta_2^2)\sigma_a^2$$
$$\gamma_1 = (\theta_1 + \theta_2\theta_1)\sigma_a^2$$
$$\gamma_2 = \theta_2\sigma_a^2$$
$$\gamma_k = 0, k > 2$$

So the a.c.f. is given by

$$\left.\begin{array}{l}\rho_1 = \dfrac{\theta_1(1 + \theta_2)}{1 + \theta_1^2 + \theta_2^2} \\[4mm] \rho_2 = \dfrac{\theta_2}{1 + \theta_1^2 + \theta_2^2} \\[4mm] \rho_k = 0, k > 2\end{array}\right\} \quad (5.5)$$

We see that the a.c.f. cuts off after lag 2. The p.a.c.f. can be shown to have no cut-off, though it decays to zero. Examples of MA(2) processes are given in *Figure 5.2*, where the four basic patterns for the $\{\rho_k\}$ and $\{\phi_{kk}\}$ are shown. These correspond to regions of invertibility identical to *Figure 4.3* on replacing ϕ_1 and ϕ_2 by $-\theta_1$ and $-\theta_2$, respectively. Again there are chance significant r_k, r_7 in (a) and r_{17} in (d). As a result of the small ρ_2 in (c) and (d), the $\{r_k\}$ may suggest

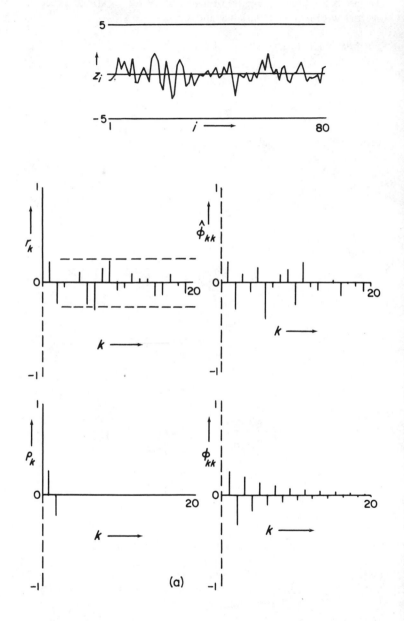

(a)

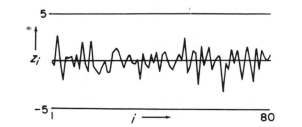

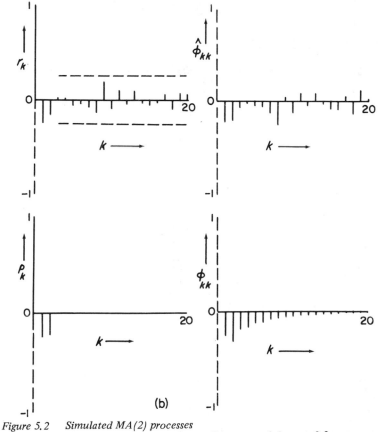

(b)

Figure 5.2   *Simulated MA(2) processes*
(a) $z_i = a_i + 0\cdot 5a_{i-1} - 0\cdot 3a_{i-2}$; *(b)* $z_i = a_i - 0\cdot 5a_{i-1} - 0\cdot 3a_{i-2}$.
((c) and (d) overleaf)

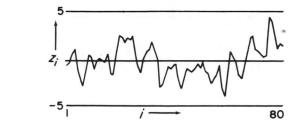

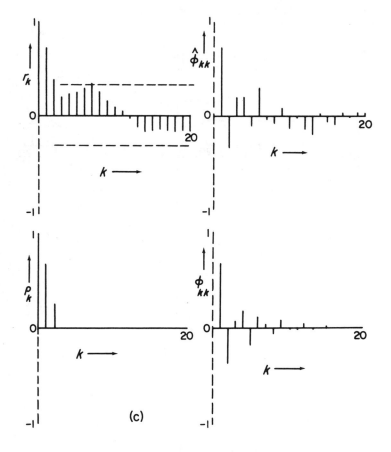

(c)

41

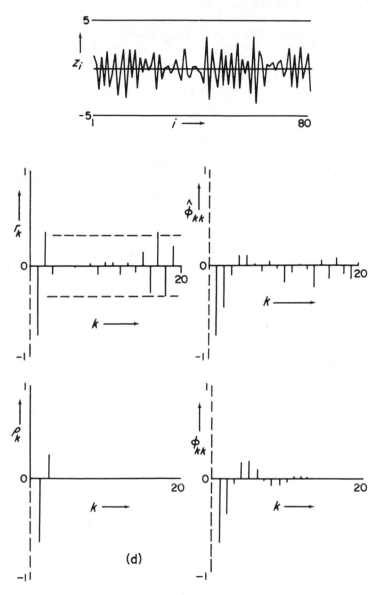

Figure 5.2   Simulated MA(2) processes (cont.)
    (c) $z_i = a_i + a_{i-1} + 0\cdot6a_{i-2}$; (d) $z_i = a_i - a_{i-1} + 0\cdot6a_{i-2}$

an MA(1) process initially, while in (*a*) and (*b*) both ρ_1 and ρ_2 are small, so $\{r_k\}$ may suggest white noise. However, it is likely that the $\{\hat{\phi}_{kk}\}$ will show values $> 2/\sqrt{N}$ in magnitude.

For the general MA(q) process, the invertibility conditions are complicated, stationarity is automatically assured, $E[z_i] = 0$ and the a.c.f. cuts off after lag q, whilst the p.a.c.f. does not cut off, but decays to zero.

We thus notice a duality between MA and AR processes, in which

$$\{\rho_k\} \text{ MA}(r) \text{ behaves similarly to } \{\phi_{kk}\} \text{ AR}(r)$$

$$\{\phi_{kk}\} \text{ MA}(r) \text{ behaves similarly to } \{\rho_k\} \text{ AR}(r) \cdot$$

Should the beginner find it difficult to remember the various general results, obtained in this and the previous chapter, it is suggested that he work out the results for the AR(1) process, from which, using a little sense and duality, the properties of the other processes follow.

Exercise 5.2 Obtain the theoretical a.c.f. for the general MA(q) process.

Solution: The method of exercise 5.1 yields

$$\rho_k = \begin{cases} \displaystyle\sum_{r=0}^{q-k} \theta_r \theta_{r+k} \Big/ \sum_{r=0}^{q} \theta_r^2 & 0 \leqslant k \leqslant q \\ 0 & k > q \end{cases} \tag{5.6}$$

where $\theta_0 = 1$.

6

Mixed Processes

A reasonable extension to the **AR** and **MA** models is the *mixed* model of the form

$$z_i = \phi_1 z_{i-1} + \ldots + \phi_p z_{i-p} + a_i + \theta_1 a_{i-1} + \ldots + \theta_q a_{i-q} \qquad (6.1)$$

called a ARMA(p,q) model, and conveniently written

$$\phi(B) z_i = \theta(B) a_i$$

Stationarity and invertibility require the zeros of $\phi(B)$ and $\theta(B)$ to lie outside the unit circle. Taking expectations in equation 6.1, $E[z_i] = 0$, since $\phi(1) \neq 0$. For any integer k, multiplying equation 6.1 by z_{i-k}, and taking expectations,

$$\gamma_k = \phi_1 \gamma_{k-1} + \ldots + \phi_p \gamma_{k-p} + \gamma_{az}(k) + \theta_1 \gamma_{az}(k-1) + \ldots$$
$$+ \theta_q \gamma_{az}(k-q) \qquad (6.2)$$

where $\gamma_{az}(j)$, the *cross covariance* between a and z at *lag difference j*, is given by

$$\gamma_{az}(j) = \text{Cov}\,[a_i, z_{i-j}]^\dagger$$

Evidently, since $E[a_i]$ and $E[z_{i-j}]$ are both zero

$$\gamma_{az}(j) = E\,[a_i z_{i-j}]$$

and an obvious property is

$$\gamma_{az}(j) = 0, \quad j > 0$$

---

†Note that, in the same notation, γ_k for z would be written $\gamma_{zz}(k)$.

43

since a_i is independent of any previous z. So for $k > q$, equation 6.2 reduces to the difference equation

$$\gamma_k = \phi_1 \, \gamma_{k-1} + \ldots + \phi_p \, \gamma_{k-p} \tag{6.3}$$

which does not involve the moving average parameters. Thus, after lag q, the autocovariances and consequently the autocorrelations behave as those for the AR process, $\phi(B) z_i = a_i$. However, for the ARMA process, the early γ_k will depend on the MA parameters through equation 6.2.

The model can be written as either

$$z_i = \psi(B)a_i$$

or

$$\pi(B) z_i = a_i$$

where $\psi(B) = \phi^{-1}(B) \theta(B)$ and $\pi(B) = \theta^{-1}(B) \phi(B)$ are infinite series in B. So, expressing the model in either MA or AR form, we are led to expect an infinite decaying p.a.c.f., as is indeed the case.

Exercise 6.1   Investigate the ARMA(1,1) process.

Solution: The model is

$$(1 - \phi B)z_i = (1 + \theta B)a_i \tag{6.4}$$

where a_i is a white noise process. For stationarity and invertibility $-1 < \phi < 1$ and $-1 < \theta < 1$. $E[z_i] = 0$, since $\phi \neq 1$. For all k,

$$\gamma_k = \phi \, \gamma_{k-1} + \gamma_{az}(k) + \theta \, \gamma_{az}(k-1)$$

so

$$\gamma_0 = \phi \, \gamma_1 + \sigma_a^2 + \theta \, \gamma_{az}(-1) \tag{6.5}$$

$$\gamma_1 = \phi \, \gamma_0 + \theta \sigma_a^2 \tag{6.6}$$

and

$$\gamma_k = \phi \, \gamma_{k-1}, \ k > 1 \tag{6.7}$$

Multiplying equation 6.4 by a_{i-1}, and taking expectations,

$$\gamma_{az}(-1) - \phi \, \sigma_a^2 = \theta \, \sigma_a^2$$

Using this to eliminate $\gamma_{az}(-1)$ from equation 6.5 and then solving
with equation 6.6, gives

$$\gamma_0 = \frac{(1 + 2\theta\phi + \theta^2)}{(1 - \phi^2)} \sigma_a^2 \qquad (6.8)$$

$$\gamma_1 = \frac{(\phi + \theta)(1 + \theta\phi)}{(1 - \phi^2)} \sigma_a^2$$

and the higher autocovariances, and so the autocorrelations, can be
determined by means of equation 6.7. Evidently the a.c.f. decays
geometrically from lag 1 onwards, like an AR(1) process with parameter ϕ.

The p.a.c.f. will decay in magnitude, with or without alternate
changes in sign, from an initial value $\phi_{11} = \rho_1$.

Figure 6.1 shows the six basic patterns for ARMA(1,1) processes,
corresponding to the six stationary-invertible regions of *Figure 6.2*.
For (a), (b), (e) and (f) there is not much structure, small magnitudes
being involved in the theoretical functions. This is due to the rough
equivalence of the AR and MA operators, and rough cancellation would
yield a white noise model. However, the realisations are likely to have
their estimated functions significantly different from white noise, as
indeed these all do. (c) and (d) have notably more structure, the two
operators being now very different, and again, in (c), there is a chance
periodic looking $\{r_k\}$.

For higher order mixed models, the a.c.f. mimics that of an AR(p)
process after $q-p$ lags, while the p.a.c.f. resembles that of an MA(q)
process after $p-q$ lags. These facts help to identify such models.

So far we have shown in our models that it is always necessary to
have $E[z_i] = 0$. This is no real restriction, since, for any stationary
time series $\{u_i\}$, we can always write $z_i = u_i - E[u_i]$.

In practice, adequate representations for many stationary series are
achieved by ARMA(p,q) models with $p + q \leqslant 2$. Since this is a book
for the beginner we will, without much loss, usually restrict our
exercises in analysis to models satisfying this inequality.

If one considers first suitably transforming a time series, for instance
by replacing z_i with $\ln z_i$[†], the scope for ARMA models can be
extended. This is also of course true for AR and MA models, which are
just special cases. Care must be taken not to over transform, and the

---

†This is an appropriate transformation for stabilising the series variance when it
increases roughly proportionally to the level — a frequent occurrence with many
series, especially in economics.

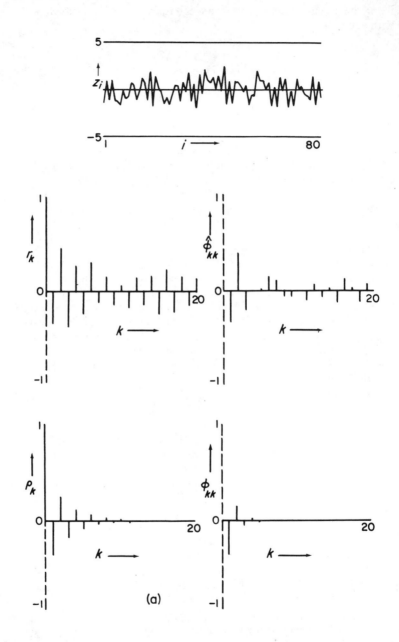

(a)

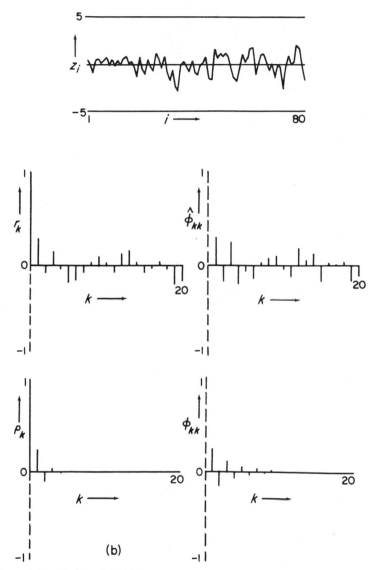

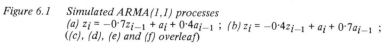

Figure 6.1   Simulated ARMA(1,1) processes
(a) $z_i = -0\cdot7z_{i-1} + a_i + 0\cdot4a_{i-1}$; (b) $z_i = -0\cdot4z_{i-1} + a_i + 0\cdot7a_{i-1}$;
((c), (d), (e) and (f) overleaf)

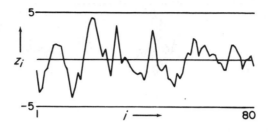

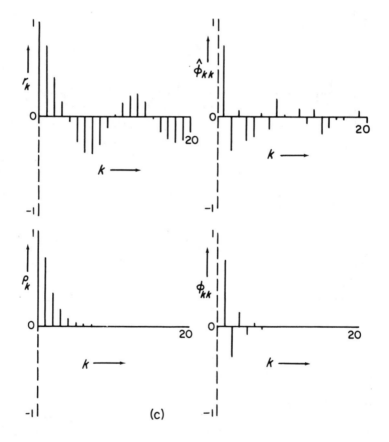

(c)

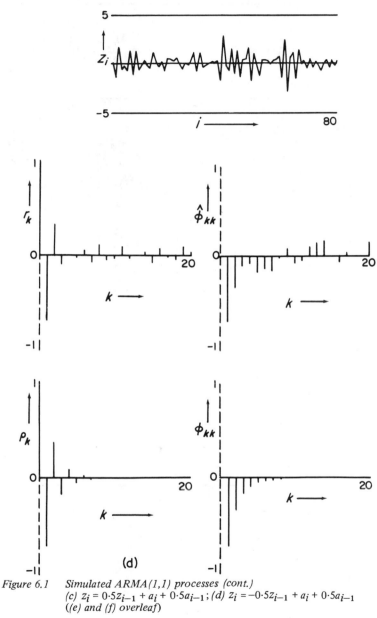

Figure 6.1   *Simulated ARMA(1,1) processes (cont.)*
(c) $z_i = 0{\cdot}5z_{i-1} + a_i + 0{\cdot}5a_{i-1}$; (d) $z_i = -0{\cdot}5z_{i-1} + a_i + 0{\cdot}5a_{i-1}$
((e) and (f) overleaf)

50

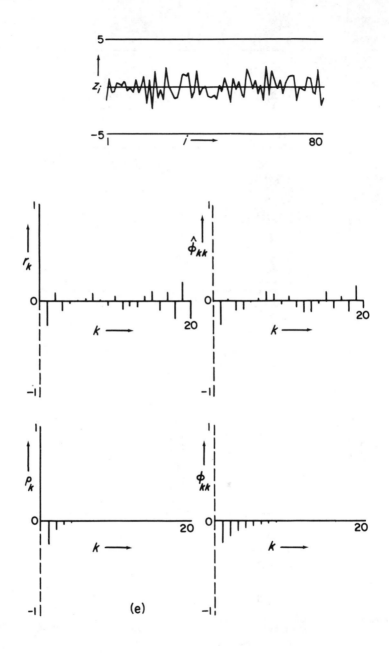

(e)

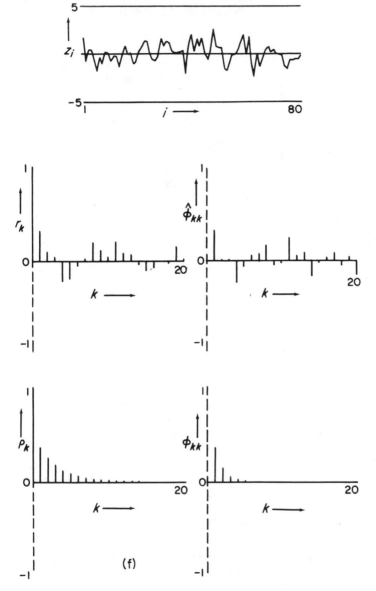

Figure 6.1   *Simulated ARMA(1,1) processes (cont.)*
     (e) $z_i = 0\cdot4z_{i-1} + a_i - 0\cdot7a_{i-1}$; (f) $z_i = 0\cdot7z_{i-1} + a_i - 0\cdot4a_{i-1}$

methodology of Box and Cox[54] is recommended. However, it should always be remembered that optimal properties, for a non-linear transform of a series, will not be optimal on transforming back to the original series.

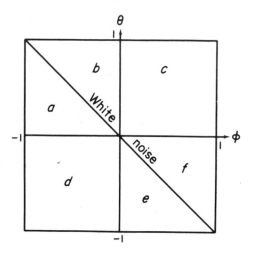

Figure 6.2   Stationary – invertible region for ARMA(1,1) processes

We have mentioned three useful alternative forms for the ARMA(p,q) model:

1. The *difference equation* form of 6.1, giving z_i in terms of the current shock and previous z and a.
2. The *random shock* form $z_i = \psi(B)a_i$, where the ψ weights are best obtained by comparing coefficients in $\phi(B)\,\psi(B) = \theta(B)$. Here z_i is given in terms of current and previous shocks.
3. Finally, we have $\pi(B)z_i = a_i$, where the π weights are obtained from $\theta(B)\,\pi(B) = \phi(B)$. This gives the *inverted* form

$$z_i = a_i + \pi_1 z_{i-1} + \pi_2 z_{i-2} + \ldots$$

with z_i in terms of the current shock and previous z.

Note that the signs, for the weights of the various polynomials in B, have been chosen systematically to be negative when the operator appears on the left, and positive when it appears on the right. Thus

$$\phi(B) \equiv (1 - \phi_1 \, B - \ldots)$$
$$\pi(B) \equiv (1 - \pi_1 \, B - \ldots)$$
$$\theta(B) \equiv (1 + \theta_1 \, B + \ldots)$$
$$\psi(B) \equiv (1 + \psi_1 \, B + \ldots)$$

Then, if the form of the model is rearranged to give

$$z_i = \text{some R.H.S.}$$

all the weights on the right are formally positive. This convention, though not standard, helps avoid confusion.

So far we have restricted ourselves to stationary processes, and the ARMA models have had all the zeros of $\phi(B)$ outside the unit circle. What happens if we relax this condition? It can be shown that, for non-stationary models with zeros *inside* the unit circle, *explosive* behaviour occurs. For instance consider $z_i = 2z_{i-1} + a_i$. So the only possibility for useful non-stationary models is for the zeros to lie *on* the unit circle, and this will be investigated in Chapters 11 and 12.

7

Identification

We now consider how the ARMA model can be *identified* for a case where it affords an adequate representation of the process generating a time series $z_1, \ldots, z_N$. The series mean, variance, a.c.f. and p.a.c.f. are calculated, and inspection of the $\{r_k\}$ and $\{\hat{\phi}_{kk}\}$ should indicate the model(s) to be entertained. This is done by considering where the cut-offs, if any, occur in the $\{\rho_k\}$ and $\{\phi_{kk}\}$, by comparing the estimated functions with their large-lag standard errors, and then seeing whether the results slot into any of the theoretical patterns. Values for p and q are thus obtained (*see Table 7.1*).

Table 7.1

$\hat{\phi}_{kk} \; \dot\sim \; N(0, \frac{1}{N}), \; k > p$	$\rightarrow$	AR(p)
$r_k \; \dot\sim \; N(0, \frac{1}{N}(1 + 2\sum_{1}^{q} r_i^2)), \; k > q$	$\rightarrow$	MA(q)
neither $\hat{\phi}_{kk}$ nor r_k cut off	$\rightarrow$	ARMA

It should be remembered that since the estimated autocorrelations are often highly correlated, $\{r_k\}$; and consequently $\{\hat{\phi}_{kk}\}$, can only be used as general guides. For instance in *Figure 6.1 (a)* and *(c)* the estimated a.c.f's do not die out as predicted. As a result of this several models might have to be fitted (*see* exercise 7.9). The identification stage thus requires (a) automatic computing and (b) intelligent inspection of the resulting output.

For a non-seasonal series, calculation of the first 20 r_k and $\hat{\phi}_{kk}$, say, is usually sufficient. The author also likes to:

1. Obtain a plot of the series, for visual inspection of its stationarity.
2. Construct a histogram of the values, to see whether a gaussian assumption is plausible.
3. Further test this assumption by obtaining the realisation skewness and kurtosis.

Should there by good reason to suspect that $E[z_i] \neq 0$, then any model would be written with $\tilde{z}_i = z_i - \bar{z}$ replacing z_i. Thus, it will often be necessary to test $E[z_i] = 0$, by comparing $\bar{z}$ with S.E. $[\bar{z}]$, which will depend on the particular process (*see Table 7.2*).

Table 7.2 Approximate Var $[\bar{z}]$ for ARMA(p,q) processes with $p+q \leqslant 2$

AR(1) $\dfrac{c_0(1-r_1)}{N(1-r_1)}$	ARMA(1,1) $\dfrac{c_0}{N}\left(1+\dfrac{2r_1^2}{r_1-r_2}\right)$	MA(1) $\dfrac{c_0(1+2r_1)}{N}$
AR(2) $\dfrac{c_0(1+r_1)(1-2r_1^2+r_2)}{N(1-r_1)(1-r_2)}$		MA(2) $\dfrac{c_0(1+2r_1+2r_2)}{N}$

Exercise 7.1 For an AR(1) process, prove S.E. $[\bar{z}] \simeq \left\{\dfrac{c_0(1+r_1)}{N(1-r_1)}\right\}^{\frac{1}{2}}$.

Solution:

$$\sigma_{\bar{z}}^2 = \frac{1}{N^2}\operatorname{Var}\left[\sum_{i=1}^{N} z_i\right]$$

$$= \frac{1}{N^2}\sum_{i=1}^{N}\sum_{j=1}^{N}\operatorname{Cov}[z_i, z_j]$$

$$= \frac{1}{N^2}\left(N\gamma_0 + 2\sum_{i,\,j>i}^{N}\gamma_{j-i}\right)$$

$$= \frac{1}{N^2}\left(N\gamma_0 + 2\sum_{k=1}^{N-1}(N-k)\gamma_k\right)$$

and assuming the a.c.f. dies out relatively quickly

$$\simeq \frac{1}{N} \sum_{-\infty}^{\infty} \gamma_k$$

$$= \frac{1}{N} \sum_{-\infty}^{\infty} \phi^{|k|} \gamma_0$$

$$= \frac{\gamma_0}{N} \left(1 + \frac{2\phi}{1-\phi}\right)$$

so

$$\hat{\sigma}_{\bar{z}}^2 \simeq \frac{c_0}{N} \left(\frac{1+\hat{\phi}}{1-\hat{\phi}}\right)$$

and

$$\text{S.E. } [\bar{z}] \simeq \left\{\frac{c_0(1+r_1)}{N(1-r_1)}\right\}^{\frac{1}{2}}$$

Having obtained a tentative model, rough values for the appropriate parameters can be found using *Table 7.3*, checking first that the r_1 and r_2 are admissible for the particular model.

Of course it is possible that an r is inadmissible owing to the corresponding ρ being near (but within) the admissible boundary, and the sampling error taking it over. As we shall see later, near non-stationarity is often best treated as non-stationarity, but near non-invertibility should not cause concern. However, being outside the admissible region does not imply that an MA process is non-invertible, but often that it is just not possible.

The author[14] has recently discovered an interesting set of inequalities, which must be obeyed by all MA processes. *For any MA (q) process, and for all integers $k \leq q$,*

$$|\rho_k| \leq \lim_{x \uparrow q} \cos\left(\frac{\pi}{\left[\frac{x+1}{k}\right] + 2}\right)$$

where $[x]$ denotes the *integer part of x*.

For instance, as is shown in Appendix III,

$$|\rho_1| \leq \cos\left(\frac{\pi}{q+2}\right)$$

Table 7.3

Process	Admissible region	Initial estimates
AR(1)	$-1 < r_1 < 1$	$\hat{\phi}_0 = r_1$
AR(2)	$-1 < r_2 < 1$	$\hat{\phi}_{1_0} = r_1(1 - r_2)/(1 - r_1^2)$
	$r_1^2 < \frac{1}{2}(r_2 + 1)$	$\hat{\phi}_{2_0} = (r_2 - r_1^2)/(1 - r_1^2)$
MA(1)	$-0.5 < r_1 < 0.5$	$\hat{\theta}_0 = \left\{1 - \sqrt{(1 - 4r_1^2)}\right\}/2r_1$
MA(2)		

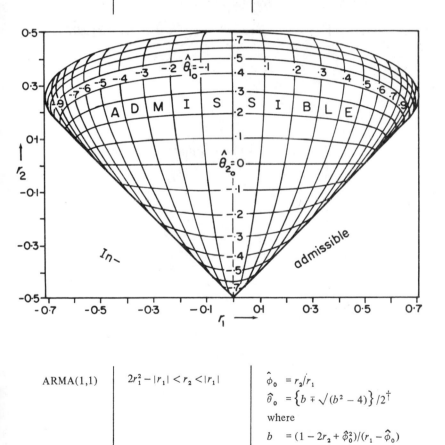

ARMA(1,1)	$2r_1^2 - \lvert r_1 \rvert < r_2 < \lvert r_1 \rvert$	$\hat{\phi}_0 = r_2/r_1$
		$\hat{\theta}_0 = \left\{b \mp \sqrt{(b^2 - 4)}\right\}/2^{\dagger}$
		where
		$b = (1 - 2r_2 + \hat{\phi}_0^2)/(r_1 - \hat{\phi}_0)$

$\dagger$ The sign being chosen to ensure $\lvert\hat{\theta}_0\rvert < 1$.

and for MA(1)

$$|\rho_1| \leqslant \tfrac{1}{2} \tag{7.1}$$

while for MA (2)

$$|\rho_1| \leqslant 1/\sqrt{2} \text{ and } |\rho_2| \leqslant \tfrac{1}{2}$$

Thus, we see that an MA(1) process cannot have ρ_1 outside the admissible region.

Exercise 7.2   Show that it is impossible for the ρ's of an MA(2) process to be (a) outside the 'box' bounded by the lines $\rho_1 = \pm 1/\sqrt{2}$, $\rho_2 = \pm \tfrac{1}{2}$ and (b) below the admissible region.

Solution: (a) follows immediately from Anderson's inequalities.
            (b) For all real a, b, c

$$(a + b + c)^2 \geqslant 0$$

So

$$a^2 + b^2 + c^2 \geqslant -2 (ab + ac + bc)$$

thus

$$-0 \cdot 5 \geqslant (ab + ac + bc)/(a^2 + b^2 + c^2)$$

and choosing first

$$a = 1, b = \theta_1, c = \theta_2$$

and then

$$a = 1, b = -\theta_1, c = \theta_2$$

it is seen, using equations 5.5, that

$$-0 \cdot 5 \geqslant \rho_2 + \rho_1 \text{ or } \rho_2 - \rho_1$$

which gives the result.

Finally, initial estimates of σ_a^2 can be obtained from

$$c_0 \left(1 - \sum_1^p \hat{\phi}_k r_k\right) \qquad \text{for AR}(p) \qquad \text{(Cf. equation 4.12)}$$

$$c_0 \Big/ \left(1 + \sum_1^q \hat{\theta}_k^2\right) \qquad \text{for MA}(q) \qquad \text{(Cf. equation 5.2)}$$

$$c_0 (1 - \hat{\phi}^2)/(1 + 2 \hat{\theta}\hat{\phi} + \hat{\theta}^2) \qquad \text{for ARMA(1,1)} \qquad \text{(Cf. equation 6.8)}$$

Exercise 7.3   When fed to a Box—Jenkins identification program, the first 200 terms of a simulated series gave the following results.

	k	1	2	3	4	5
$\bar{z} = 0.03$	r_k	−0·800	0·670	−0·518	0·390	−0·310
$s_z^2 = 3.34$	$\hat{\phi}_{kk}$	−0·800	0·085	0·112	−0·046	−0·061

and *see Figure 7.1 (a)*.

What conclusions can be drawn?

Solution: $2/\sqrt{N} = 0.1414$

$\{r_k\}$ disqualifies the possibility of an MA process.

$\{\hat{\phi}_{kk}\}$ very strongly suggests an AR(1) process.

S.E. $[\bar{z}]$ = $\left(\dfrac{3\cdot34 \times 0\cdot2}{200 \times 1\cdot8}\right)^{\frac{1}{2}}$ = 0·136, so $\bar{z}$ is not significantly different from zero. Initial parameter estimates, $\hat{\phi}_0 = -0\cdot80$, $\hat{\sigma}_a^2 = 3\cdot34\,(1-0\cdot8^2) =$ 1·20. So initial model is

$$z_i = -0\cdot80\, z_{i-1} + a_i, a_i \sim IN(0, 1\cdot20)$$

In fact, the series was an extension of the AR(1) simulation in *Figure 4.1(a)*. Note that, for the longer series, the estimated functions are closer to the theoretical ones. This is to be expected since the standard errors decrease with increasing N, but one should not normally expect to get such an accurate initial model.

Exercise 7.4   Interpret the following Box—Jenkins analysis.

	k	1	2	3	4	5
$N = 200$						
$\bar{z} = -0.34$	r_k	0·449	−0·056	−0·023	0·028	0·013
$s_z^2 = 1.34$	$\hat{\phi}_{kk}$	0·449	−0·324	0·218	−0·118	0·077

and *see Figure 7.1 (b)*.

Solution: $\{r_k\}$ suggests MA(1). $\{\hat{\phi}_{kk}\}$ seems compatible with this. However, assuming an MA(1), Bartlett's formula shows that, for $k > 1$, S.E. $[r_k]$ = 0·084, and four of the later r_k would be significant. Perhaps, in consequence, the only open alternative of an ARMA(1,1)

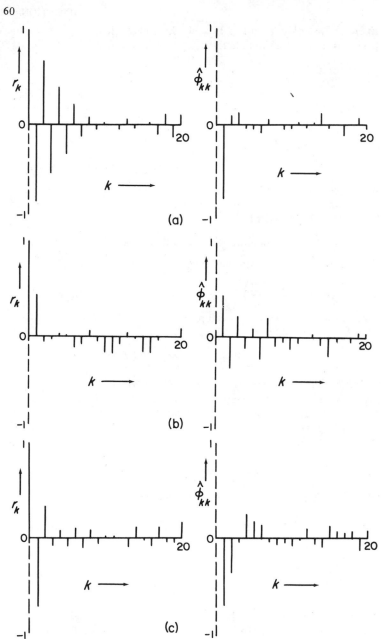

(a)

(b)

(c)

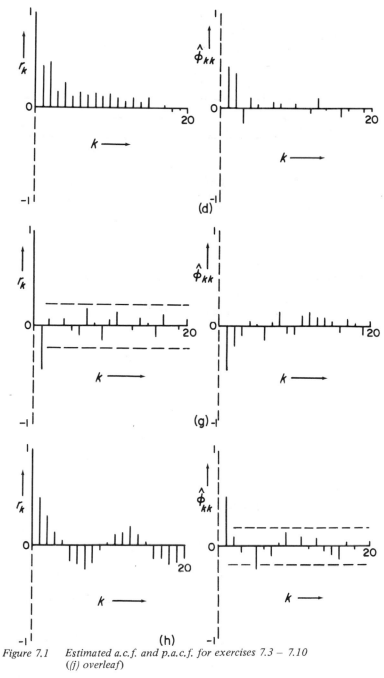

Figure 7.1   Estimated a.c.f. and p.a.c.f. for exercises 7.3 − 7.10
((j) overleaf)

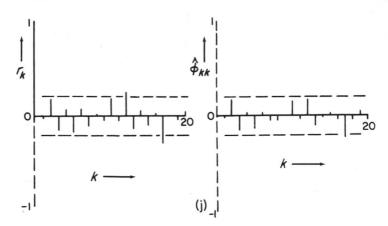

should be investigated. But for the sake of parsimony, we will initially consider an MA(1) model.

$$\text{S.E.}[\bar{z}] = \left\{\frac{1\cdot34}{200}\ (1 + 2 \times 0\cdot449)\right\}^{\frac{1}{2}} = 0\cdot113, \text{ so } \bar{z} \text{ is significantly}$$

different from zero.

$$\hat{\theta}_0 = \left\{1 - \sqrt{(1 - 4 \times 0\cdot449^2)}\right\}/(2 \times 0\cdot449) = 0\cdot62$$
$$\hat{\sigma}_a^2 = 1\cdot34/(1 + 0\cdot624^2) = 0\cdot96$$

So initial MA(1) model is

$$z_i = -0\cdot34 + a_i + 0\cdot62\ a_{i-1}, a_i \sim IN(0, 0\cdot96)$$

The series was another simulation of $z_i = a_i + 0\cdot8\ a_{i-1}$ (cf. *Figure 5.1(b)*), and the initial model is nowhere near so good this time.

Exercise 7.5   Identify the process giving the following results.

$N = 200$	k	1	2	3	4	5
$\bar{z} = -0\cdot05$	r_k	$-0\cdot719$	$0\cdot337$	$-0\cdot083$	$0\cdot075$	$-0\cdot088$
$s_z^2 = 2\cdot32$	$\hat{\phi}_{kk}$	$-0\cdot719$	$-0\cdot375$	$-0\cdot048$	$0\cdot239$	$0\cdot173$

and *see Figure 7.1(c)*.

Solution: $\{r_k\}$ suggests MA(2). $\{\hat{\phi}_{kk}\}$ compatible with this. Unfortunately r_1, r_2 are then inadmissible. The only open alternative is

ARMA$(1,1)$ and r_1, r_2 are admissible for this, since

$$(2 \times 0.517) - 0.719 = 0.315 < 0.337 < 0.719$$

So, for ARMA $(1,1)$,

$$\hat{\phi}_0 = 0.337/-0.719 = -0.47$$
$$b = (1 - 2 \times 0.337 + 0.4687^2)/(-0.719 + 0.4687) = 2.180$$

and

$$\hat{\theta}_0 = \{-2.180 + \sqrt{(2.180^2 - 4)}\}/2 = -0.66$$

the positive sign being chosen, since the negative sign would lead to a non-invertible model.

$$\hat{\sigma}_a = 2.32 \, (1 - 0.4687^2)/(1 + 0.6563^2 + 2 \times 0.4687 \times 0.6563) = 0.88$$

Finally,

$$\text{S.E. } [\bar{z}] = \left\{ \frac{2.32}{200} \left(1 + \frac{2 \times 0.719^2}{-0.719 - 0.337}\right) \right\}^{\frac{1}{2}} = 0.016$$

so $\bar{z}$, though small, is significant.
    Thus initial model is

$$z_i = -0.05 - 0.47\, z_{i-1} + a_i - 0.66\, a_{i-1}, a_i \sim IN(0, 0.88)$$

The generating process was $z_i = a_i - a_{i-1} + 0.6\, a_{i-2}$ (cf. *Figure 5.2(d)*), so the identified model is very inaccurate. However, if the inadmissibility of r_1 and r_2 had been ignored, an MA(2) process would have been (correctly) entertained. This will be considered further in exercise 9.3.

Exercise 7.6   Identify a possible generating process for the following results.

$N = 200$	k	1	2	3	4	5
$\bar{z} = 0.09$	r_k	0.427	0.475	0.169	0.253	0.126
$s_z^2 = 1.15$	$\hat{\phi}_{kk}$	0.427	0.358	-0.160	0.106	0.035

and *see Figure 7.1(d)*.

Solution: $\{r_k\}$ disqualifies MA process. $\hat{\phi}_{33}$ is just significant, if it is ignored an AR(2) is possible, otherwise *our* only choice is ARMA$(1,1)$.

$$\text{AR(2)}\quad \text{S.E. } [\bar{z}] = \left\{ \frac{1\cdot15 \times 1\cdot427\,(1-2\times 0\cdot427^2 + 0\cdot475)}{200 \times 0\cdot573 \times 0\cdot525} \right\}^{\frac{1}{2}} = 0\cdot174$$

so $\bar{z}$ is not significant.

$$\hat{\phi}_{1_0} = 0\cdot427 \times 0\cdot525/(1 - 0\cdot427^2) = 0\cdot27$$

$$\hat{\phi}_{2_0} = (0\cdot475 - 0\cdot427^2)/(1 - 0\cdot427^2) = 0\cdot36$$

$$\hat{\sigma}_a^2 = 1\cdot15\,(1 - 0\cdot2742 \times 0\cdot427 - 0\cdot3579 \times 0\cdot475) = 0\cdot82$$

So initial AR(2) model is

$$z_i = 0\cdot27\,z_{i-1} + 0\cdot36 z_{i-2} + a_i, a_i \sim IN(0, 0\cdot82)$$

ARMA(1,1) $r_2 \not< |r_1|$ so model is inadmissible.

Exercise 7.7   For each of *Figures 4.1, 4.2, 5.1, 5.2* and *6.1*, identify the (*b*) process from its estimated a.c.f. and p.a.c.f.

Solution: *Figure 4.1(b)*: $\{r_k\}$ disqualifies MA process. $\{\hat{\phi}_{kk}\}$ strongly suggests AR(1). $\hat{\phi}_0 = 0\cdot88$, so identified model is

$$z_i = 0\cdot88\,z_{i-1} + a_i$$

Figure 4.2 (b): $\{r_k\}$ disqualifies MA, $\{\hat{\phi}_{kk}\}$ suggests AR(2), (though $\hat{\phi}_{55}$ is about significant).

$$\hat{\phi}_{1_0} = \frac{0\cdot48\,(1 - 0\cdot49)}{1 - 0\cdot48^2} = 0\cdot32 \text{ and } \hat{\phi}_{2_0} = \frac{0\cdot49 - 0\cdot48^2}{1 - 0\cdot48^2} = 0\cdot34$$

So initial model is

$$z_i = 0\cdot32\,z_{i-1} + 0\cdot34\,z_{i-2} + a_i$$

Figure 5.1(b): $\{r_k\}$ suggests MA(1), $\{\hat{\phi}_{kk}\}$ is compatible with this. $r_1 = 0\cdot62 > \rho_{1\,max}$ for MA(1) from inequality 7.1, so take $r_1 = 0\cdot5$ (or perhaps MA(2) with small ρ_2), which implies that initial model is

$$z_i = a_i + a_{i-1}$$

Figure 5.2 (b): There is little structure. However $\hat{\phi}_{11}, \hat{\phi}_{88} > 2/\sqrt{80}$ and the general pattern of $\{\hat{\phi}_{kk}\}$ suggests that $\{\phi_{kk}\}$ is mostly negative. r_1 is the only appreciable r_k, so an MA(1) is plausible.

$$\hat{\theta}_0 = \{1 - \sqrt{(1 - 4 \times 0\cdot24^2)}\}\,/-0\cdot48 = -0\cdot26$$

So initial model is

$$z_i = a_i - 0\cdot26\,a_{i-1}$$

Figure 6.1 (b): Neither $\{r_k\}$ nor $\{\hat{\phi}_{kk}\}$ have much structure. However $r_1 > 2/\sqrt{80}$, as are $\hat{\phi}_{11}$ and $\hat{\phi}_{33}$, which suggests ARMA(1,1) with roughly equivalent operators. $r_1 = 0{\cdot}28$, $r_2 = -0{\cdot}08$ so $\hat{\phi}_0 = -0{\cdot}29$, $b = 2{\cdot}19$ and $\hat{\theta}_0 = 0{\cdot}65$. Thus initial model is

$$z_i = -0{\cdot}29z_{i-1} + a_i + 0{\cdot}65a_{i-1}$$

Exercise 7.8   Carry out a Box–Jenkins identification of series G, enumerated in Appendix I. (The program in Appendix II may help, but if you do not wish to become involved with computing yet, just interpret the given output).

Solution: The series is pictured in *Figure 7.2 (g)*, and appears to be stationary. $\bar{z} = 0{\cdot}01$, $s_z^2 = 1{\cdot}16$, $2/\sqrt{N} = 0{\cdot}2$, and the estimated a.c.f. and p.a.c.f. are shown in *Figure 7.1 (g)*. $\{r_k\}$ suggests MA(1), $\{\hat{\phi}_{kk}\}$ is compatible with this. $\{\hat{\phi}_{kk}\}$ is also compatible with an AR process, but $\{r_k\}$ disqualifies the possibility.

$$\hat{\theta}_0 = \left\{1 - \sqrt{(1 - 4 \times 0{\cdot}470^2)}\right\}/(2 \times 0{\cdot}470) = -0{\cdot}70$$

$$\hat{\sigma}_a^2 = 1{\cdot}16/(1 + 0{\cdot}701^2) = 0{\cdot}78$$

S.E. $[\bar{z}] = \left\{1{\cdot}16(1 + 2 \times -0{\cdot}470)/100\right\}^{1/2} = 0{\cdot}03$, so z is not significant. Thus initial model is

$$z_i = a_i - 0{\cdot}70a_{i-1}, \; a_i \sim IN(0, 0{\cdot}78)$$

In fact series G was obtained by rounding the values of a simulated MA(1) series with parameter $-0{\cdot}6$ and standardised normal shocks. As will be seen (*Table 8.1*), for 100 terms the difference between $-0{\cdot}7$ and $-0{\cdot}6$ is not significant.

Exercise 7.9   Identify series H (Appendix I).

Solution: *See Figures 7.2 (h)* and *7.1 (h)*. $\bar{z} = -0{\cdot}08$, $s_z^2 = 1{\cdot}42$. $\{r_k\}$ disqualifies an MA process. If $\hat{\phi}_{55}$ is considered as just a chance significant value, $\{\hat{\phi}_{kk}\}$ is compatible with an AR(1) model. If, however, this is not accepted, $\{\hat{\phi}_{kk}\}$ is not compatible with a low order AR, and restricting ourselves to $(p+q) \leqslant 2$, we entertain an ARMA(1,1) model. Thus there are two possibilities, though if the reader finds them both acceptable, the principle of parsimony should decide him to try first the AR(1).

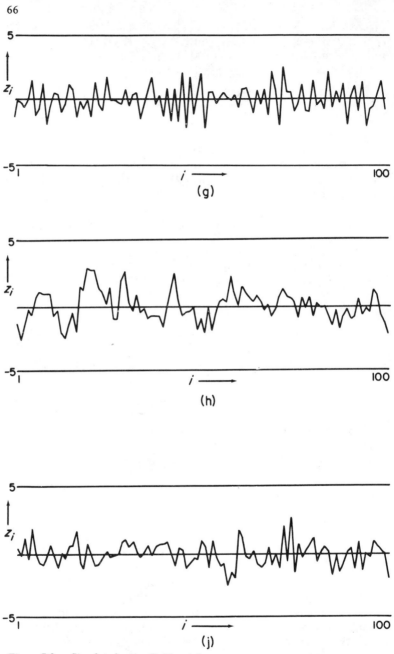

Figure 7.2   Simulated series G, H and J

AR(1) $\hat{\phi}_0 = 0.50$, $\hat{\sigma}_a^2 = 1.42\,(1 - 0.499^2) = 1.07$

S.E. $[\bar{z}] = \left\{ \dfrac{1.42\,(1 + 0.499)}{100\,(1 - 0.499)} \right\}^{\frac{1}{2}} = 0.21$, so $\bar{z}$ is not significant.

So initial AR(1) model is

$$z_i = 0.50\,z_{i-1} + a_i, \; a_i \sim IN(0, 1.07)$$

ARMA(1,1) $\hat{\phi}_0 = 0.308/0.499 = 0.62$

$b = (1 - 2 \times 0.308 + 0.6172^2)/(0.499 - 0.6172) = -6.472$

$\therefore \quad \hat{\theta}_0 = \{-6.471 + \sqrt{(41.87 - 4)}\}/2 = -0.16$

$\hat{\sigma}_a^2 = 1.42\,(1 - 0.6172^2)/$
$\qquad (1 + 0.1585^2 - 2 \times 0.6172 \times 0.1585) = 0.83$

S.E. $[\bar{z}] = \left\{ \dfrac{1.42}{100} \left(1 + \dfrac{2 \times 0.499^2}{0.499 - 0.308} \right) \right\}^{\frac{1}{2}} = 0.23,$

so $\bar{z}$ is not significant.

So initial ARMA(1,1) model is

$$z_i = 0.62\,z_{i-1} + a_i - 0.16\,a_{i-1}, \; a_i \sim IN(0, 0.83)$$

Multiplying the AR(1) model through by $(1 - 0.12B)$ gives

$$z_i = 0.62\,z_{i-1} - 0.06\,z_{i-2} + a_i - 0.12\,a_{i-1}$$

so the two initial models are close, as might have been expected if the process were actually AR(1).

Exercise 7.10 Identify series J (Appendix I).

Solution: *See Figures 7.2 (j) and 7.1 (j).* $\bar{z} = -0.12$, $s_z^2 = 0.84$. $\{r_k\}$ and $\{\hat{\phi}_{kk}\}$ have no early significant terms, which suggests white noise.

S.E. $[\bar{z}] = 0.092$, so z is not significant. Thus initial model is

$$z_i = a_i, \; a_i \sim IN(0, 0.84)$$

The series in these exercises were all simulated from ARMA(p,q) models with $p, q \leqslant 2$, and series encountered in practice are not likely to behave so well. Even here we have not managed to identify the actual model each time. Some experience of identifying models for naturally occurring series will be obtained in Chapters 11 and 12.

8

Estimation

Having identified a tentative model, the next stage is to estimate its parameters efficiently using the rough values, calculated at the identification stage, as initial values. Box and Jenkins[2] discuss how this can be done, though this is not work for the beginner. A *non-linear least squares* procedure is used to obtain the vector of parameter estimates

$$(\hat{\phi}, \hat{\theta}) \equiv (\hat{\phi}_1, \ldots, \hat{\phi}_p, \hat{\theta}_1, \ldots, \hat{\theta}_q)$$

which minimises the *shock sum of squares*

$$S(\phi, \theta) = \sum_1^N \alpha_i^2$$

where the $\alpha_i = \theta^{-1}(B) \phi(B) z_i$ are the *estimated shocks* given the model and the series. Box and Jenkins give a rather vague description of such a program, but satisfactory packages are now becoming available, for instance I.C.L.[15]

The $\{\alpha_i\}$ which minimise S are written $\{\hat{a}_i\}$ and are called the *residuals* by most authors. This term implies

$$\hat{a}_i = z_i - \hat{z}_i \qquad (8.1)$$

a result which seems far from obvious.

Proof: Writing the fitted model in inverted form

$$z_i = \hat{a}_i + \hat{\pi}_1 z_{i-1} + \ldots$$

yields equation 8.1 on noting that

$$\hat{z}_i = \hat{\pi}_1, z_{i-1} + \ldots$$

To emphasise these two ways of interpreting the $\hat{a}_i$'s, we will call them the *shock estimates* for this and the next chapter.

68

Alternatively, a *grid-search* method can be used. A neighbourhood of the initial estimates vector, within the stationary invertible region, is first chosen, and a fine mesh of points superimposed. The estimated shocks, for models with parameters at the mesh points, are calculated, and the S contours plotted. From these, the point corresponding to the minimum of the S surface can generally be determined with precision, and this is taken as the vector estimate.

For a single parameter model, the S surface is merely a curve, and for not more than two parameters in the model (which covers all the cases we are usually considering), the surface can be readily represented. For more than two parameters, a multitude of plots, each holding all but two parameters constant, is necessary, and the technique is less convenient. The advantage of the method is that the S surface, for varying parameters, can be studied visually, and it often provides useful information.

In fact, Box and Jenkins[2] recommend that the S surface be always plotted in any new investigation, since this ensures that any peculiarities in the estimation situation are shown up, and prevents, for instance, homing in on a minor dip in the surface.

Consider the problem of estimating ARMA (p,q) given $z_1, \ldots, z_N$, where as usual, if $E[Z] \neq 0$, z is replaced by $\tilde{z} = z - E[Z]$, and for a moderately long series $\bar{z}$ can be safely substituted for $E[Z]$. The estimated shocks are connected by

$$\alpha_i = z_i + \phi_1 z_{i-1} + \ldots + \phi_p z_{i-p} + \theta_1 \alpha_{i-1} + \ldots + \theta_q \alpha_{i-q}$$

where the α's need to be calculated. But to obtain α_1 requires knowledge of $\alpha_0, \ldots, \alpha_{1-q}$ and $z_0, \ldots, z_{i-p}$ (α^* and z^*, say) which is not available. So $\alpha_1, \ldots, \alpha_N$ can only be obtained conditional on giving α^* and z^* certain values, when they are written as $\alpha_1^*, \ldots, \alpha_N^*$.

The problem is to choose these *starting* values. Two possibilities are proposed, when N is moderate or large:

1. Put all starting values equal to zero, their unconditional expectation. This will give a good approximation provided none of the AR zeros are near the unit circle. However, if this condition does not hold, z_1 can deviate considerably from 0, when $\alpha_1 = z_1$ would be considerable, and a large transient, slow to die out, might be introduced. Under these circumstances it is better to:
2. Just calculate α_{p+1} onwards, putting $\alpha_1, \ldots, \alpha_p = 0$, when only actually occurring z_i enter the calculation. S has then lost p of its N terms, but this slight loss of information will generally be unimportant for a longish series. Of course if $p = 0$, (1) and (2) are the same.

Example: For z_i identified as MA(1)

$$\alpha_i = z_i - \theta\,\alpha_{i-1}, \qquad i = 1, \ldots, N$$

Put $\alpha_0 = 0$, then $\alpha_1{}^* = z_1, \alpha_2{}^* = z_2 - \theta\,\alpha_1^*, \ldots, \alpha_N{}^* = z_N - \theta\alpha_{N-1}^*$,

and the conditional S, $S^*\,(\theta) = \displaystyle\sum_1^N \alpha_i^{*2}$. $S^*\,(\theta)$ is then plotted

against θ, and the minimum obtained.

When even (2) is not sufficient, the starting values are obtained by *backcasting*[2], a method by which the forecasting discussed in Chapter 10 is used on the reversed series to estimate its values before observation began.

Approximate standard errors for the parameter estimates of the various simple models can be obtained from *Table 8.1*[2].

Table 8.1 Approximate variances for parameter estimates of simple models

AR(1)	$\mathrm{Var}[\hat\phi] \simeq \dfrac{1-\phi^2}{N}$
AR(2)	$\mathrm{Var}[\hat\phi_1], \quad \mathrm{Var}[\hat\phi_2] \simeq \dfrac{1-\phi_2^2}{N}$
MA(1)	$\mathrm{Var}[\hat\theta] \simeq \dfrac{1-\theta^2}{N}$
MA(2)	$\mathrm{Var}[\hat\theta_1], \quad \mathrm{Var}[\hat\theta_2] \simeq \dfrac{1-\theta_2^2}{N}$
ARMA(1,1)	$\mathrm{Var}[\hat\phi] \simeq \dfrac{(1-\phi^2)}{N}\dfrac{(1+\phi\theta)^2}{(\phi+\theta)^2}$
	$\mathrm{Var}[\hat\theta] \simeq \dfrac{(1-\theta^2)}{N}\dfrac{(1+\phi\theta)^2}{(\phi+\theta)^2}$

Note that, for example, one cannot obtain $\mathrm{Var}[\hat\phi]$ for AR(1) by putting $\phi_2 = 0$ in $\mathrm{Var}[\hat\phi_1]$ for AR(2).

When $\phi = -\theta$, the variances for the ARMA(1,1) model are infinite. This is because the AR and MA operators cancel to leave $z_i = a_i$, which can provide no information on the common parameter value. Such *parameter redundancy* is avoided by rejecting any model for which the initial estimates show an approximately common factor in both operators. Consequently, an identified model $(1-\phi B)z_i = (1 + \theta B)a_i$ with $\hat{\phi}_0 = 0.7$, $\hat{\theta}_0 = -0.6$, say, would be abandoned, unless it was based on a sufficiently long series.

Redundancy is not so obvious with higher order models, but will be avoided by sensible parsimonious preliminary identification. For instance, the model

$$(1 - 1.2B + 0.32B^2)\, z_i = (1 - 0.3B)\, a_i$$

can be written

$$(1 - 0.8B)\,(1 - 0.4B)\, z_i = (1 - 0.3B)\, a_i$$

with a near common factor. But it can also be written as

$$(1 - 0.9B + 0.05B^2 + \ldots)\, z_i = a_i$$

which is very close to an AR(1) representation. The principle of parsimony would in practice have caused an AR(1) rather than AR(2,1) model to be fitted.

Exercise 8.1 The following values were obtained when the simulated series $z_i = a_i - 0.8a_{i-1}$, $a_i \sim IN(0,1)$ shown in *Figure 5.1(a)* was subjected to efficient estimation.

    Shock variance $\hat{\sigma}_a^2 = 0.946$

    Parameter estimate $\hat{\theta} = -0.759$ with S.E. $= 0.0714$. Check the compatibility of these statistics with the generating process.

Solution: $1/\hat{\sigma}_a^2 = 1.057$, $F_{\infty, 78_5\%} > 1.25$, so $\hat{\sigma}_a^2$ is not significantly different from 1.
Table 8.1 gives $\mathrm{Var}(\hat{\theta}) \simeq \dfrac{1 - 0.5761}{80} = 0.0053 = 0.0728^2$, so S.E.

appears to be correct.
Finally, $\hat{\theta} - \theta = 0.041 <$ S.E., so it is not significant. Thus the realisation seems compatible with the generating process.

Exercise 8.2 Give rough 95% confidence intervals for the shock variance and the parameters in an identified ARMA(1,1) series of length 121, with efficient estimates

$$\hat{\sigma}_a^2 = 0.097, \quad \hat{\phi} = 0.92, \quad \hat{\theta} = -0.58$$

Solution: $\quad p\left(\dfrac{1}{1.31} < \dfrac{\hat{\sigma}_a^2}{\sigma_a^2} < 1.31\right) \simeq 0.95$

so approximate confidence interval (C.I.) given by $0 \cdot 074 < \sigma_a^2 < 0 \cdot 127$.

$$\text{S.E. } [\hat{\phi}] = \left\{ \frac{(1 - 0 \cdot 92^2)}{121} \frac{(1 - 0 \cdot 92 \times 0 \cdot 58)^2}{(0 \cdot 92 - 0 \cdot 58)^2} \right\}^{1/2} = 0 \cdot 049$$

$$\text{S.E. } [\hat{\theta}] = \left\{ \frac{(1 - 0 \cdot 58^2)}{121} \frac{(1 - 0 \cdot 92 \times 0 \cdot 58)^2}{(0 \cdot 92 - 0 \cdot 58)^2} \right\}^{1/2} = 0 \cdot 102$$

So approximate C.I's given by $0 \cdot 82 < \phi < 1 \cdot 02$

and $-0 \cdot 78 < \theta < -0 \cdot 38$

Exercise 8.3   If a program is available, efficiently estimate the parameters in the model identified for series G in exercise 7.8. (Keep your output for later exercises).

Solution: $\hat{\sigma}_a^2 = 0 \cdot 872$, $\hat{\theta} = -0 \cdot 465$, S.E.$[\hat{\theta}] = 0 \cdot 090$ ($\hat{\theta}$, though further than $\hat{\theta}_0$ from $-0 \cdot 6$, is still not significantly different from it).

Exercise 8.4   In exercise 7.9, two possible models were suggested for series H. When fitted efficiently these gave:

AR(1)	$\hat{\phi} = 0 \cdot 516$	S.E.$[\hat{\phi}] = 0 \cdot 086$	$\hat{\sigma}_a^2 = 1 \cdot 046$
ARMA(1,1)	$\hat{\phi} = 0 \cdot 638$	S.E.$[\hat{\phi}] = 0 \cdot 151$	
	$\hat{\theta} = -0 \cdot 176$	S.E.$[\hat{\theta}] = 0 \cdot 195$	$\hat{\sigma}_a^2 = 1 \cdot 034$

Comment.

Solution: $F_{98,97_5 \%} > 1 \cdot 25$, so the two estimates of σ_a^2 are nothing like significantly different, though this test is rather bogus, since the estimates are *not* independent. (In future, in such a situation, we will use the term *substantial* rather than significant). Further, for the ARMA fit, $\hat{\theta}$ is not significant, $\hat{\phi}$ is not significantly different from the parameter of the AR fit, and it seems likely that a joint significance test would not distinguish between the two models. Consequently, there is no real evidence for preferring ARMA(1,1) to the more parsimonious AR(1).

Also note that $(1 - 0 \cdot 52B) z_i = a_i$, when multiplied by $(1 - 0 \cdot 12B)$ gives $(1 - 0 \cdot 64B + 0 \cdot 06B^2) z_i = (1 - 0 \cdot 12B) a_i$, which is close to the ARMA(1,1) fit. The rough parameter redundancy is reflected in the much larger S.E's of the ARMA fit, (and in fact the ARMA fit was unstable).

Actually, series H was a simulation of

$$z_i = 0.6\, z_{i-1} + a_i - 0.2\, a_{i-1}, \; \sigma_a^2 = 1$$

with its values rounded to two decimal places, so the ARMA fit was not far out. However, for a realisation of length only 100, the extra 'resolution' required to distinguish the ARMA model from its AR approximation is just not there.

Exercise 8.5 If a program is available, obtain efficient estimates for an AR(2) fit to series K of Appendix I (keep your output).

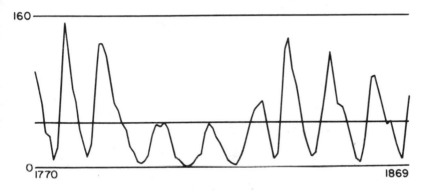

Figure 8.1   Series K: Wölfer annual sunspot numbers

Solution: A plot of the series is given in *Figure 8.1*. The AR(2) pattern that the series most closely resembles is that illustrated in *Figure 4.2(d)*, so we may as well start with

$$\hat{\phi}_{1_0} = 1, \; \hat{\phi}_{2_0} = -0.6$$

and avoid estimating ρ_1, ρ_2. From a practical point of view, the mean level is obviously greater than zero, so we work with $\tilde{z}_i = z_i - \bar{z}$.
Efficient estimation then gives $\hat{\sigma}_a^2 = 227.5$

$$\hat{\phi}_1 = 1.403, \; \text{S.E.}[\hat{\phi}_1] = 0.071$$

$$\hat{\phi}_2 = -0.710, \text{S.E.}[\hat{\phi}_2] = 0.070$$

$\bar{z} = 46.93$, so estimated fit is

$$z_i = 14.41 + 1.40\, z_{i-1} - 0.71 z_{i-2} + a_i$$

where $a_i \sim IN(0, 228)$.

From now on, we refer to pure AR and MA models as *simple* models, and denote white noise by w.n. An immediate question, raised by exercise 8.4, is 'When can an ARMA(1,1) model be replaced by an equivalent simple model?'

Consider

$$(1 - \phi B)z_i = (1 + \theta B)a_i$$

This can be written

$$z_i = \quad (1 + \phi B + \phi^2 B^2 + \ldots)(1 + \theta B)a_i$$

$$(1 + \phi B)(1 + \theta B)a_i \quad \text{when } \phi \text{ small}$$

$$\simeq \quad \{1 + (\phi + \theta)B\}\, a_i \quad \text{when } \phi \text{ and } \theta \text{ small}$$

$$a_i \quad \text{when } (\phi + \theta) \text{ very small}$$

Alternatively

$$(1 - \theta B + \theta^2 B^2 - \ldots)(1 - \phi B)z_i = a_i$$

so

$$(1 - \theta B)(1 - \phi B)\, z_i \quad \text{when } \theta \text{ small}$$

$$\{1 - (\theta + \phi)B\} z_i \simeq a_i \quad \text{when } \theta \text{ and } \phi \text{ small}$$

$$z_i \quad \text{when } (\theta + \phi) \text{ very small}$$

Thus, if the sum of the ARMA parameters is very small, the process is effectively w.n., while if one or both of the parameters are small, the process is roughly equivalent to a simple one.

It is also clear that for an ARMA(1,1) model, a small change in one of θ or ϕ can be nearly compensated by a suitable change in the other. This can cause difficulty in estimation.

9

Verification

The final stage of the Box–Jenkins cycle is to subject the identified and estimated model to *diagnostic checks* of its adequacy. Such checks should be designed to test for any suspected departures from the *fit*, and also to show up any other serious discrepancies. When an inadequacy is detected, the checks should give an indication of how the model need be modified, after which further fitting and checking takes place.

If we suspect a more elaborate model might be necessary, we can *overfit* another model with extra parameters, and then see whether this model is indeed superior. The ARMA(1,1) of exercise 8.4 can be considered as an unaccepted overfit to the initially chosen parsimonious AR(1). It would, however, be foolish to increase the orders of the AR and MA operators simultaneously, since this could lead to parameter redundancy. For instance if we tried to fit an ARMA(1,1) as an overfit to the w.n. model of exercise 7.10, we would run into extreme parameter instability, owing to the high variances which resulted.

Exercise 9.1 In exercise 7.4, although an MA(1) was identified, it was suggested that the process could be ARMA(1,1).
The efficient fit and overfit gave:

Model	Parameter estimates	S.E's of estimates	$\hat{\sigma}_a^2$	χ^2
MA(1)	$\hat{\theta} = 0.845$	0.038	0.833	22.45
ARMA(1,1)	$\hat{\phi} = -0.004$	0.082		
	$\hat{\theta} = 0.851$	0.041	0.830	21.77

Ignoring the χ^2 column, for the present, what can be concluded?

Solution: The overfit does not substantially decrease the shock variance. The overfit has parameters which are not significantly different from those of the fit. So the overfit is not justified.

Incidently, an MA(2) overfit gave

$$\hat{\theta}_1 = 0.824 \quad S.E.[\hat{\theta}_1] = 0.068$$

$$\hat{\theta}_2 = -0.026 \quad S.E.[\hat{\theta}_2] = 0.070 \quad \hat{\sigma}_a^2 = 0.831 \quad \chi^2 = 21.00$$

and so this unintelligent overfit would also be rejected. (In fact the series was a simulation of $z_i = a_i + 0.8a_{i-1}$).

Exercise 9.2 For series G, of exercises 7.8 and 8.3, overfit MA(2) and ARMA(1,1) models, and comment.

Solution: Again ignoring the χ^2 column, efficient estimation gives:

Model	Parameter estimates	S.E's of estimates	$\hat{\sigma}_a^2$	χ^2
MA(1)	$\hat{\theta} = -0.465$	0.090	0.872	14.33
MA(2)	$\hat{\theta}_1 = -0.551$	0.097		
	$\hat{\theta}_2 = 0.146$	0.101	0.863	15.24
ARMA(1,1)	$\hat{\phi} = -0.216$	0.191		
	$\hat{\theta} = -0.331$	0.195	0.849	17.98

The MA(2) parameters are not significantly different from those of the MA(1), nor is the shock variance substantially reduced. So the MA(2) overfit is not justified.

The same holds for the ARMA(1,1) which can also be written

$$z_i = (1 + 0.216B)^{-1}(1 - 0.331B)a_i$$

$$= (1 - 0.547B + 0.118B^2 - 0.026B^3 + \ldots)a_i$$

$$\simeq (1 - 0.55B + 0.12B^2)a_i$$

As expected, neither overfit is justified.

Exercise 9.3 The series in exercise 7.5 was in fact generated by an MA(2) process, $z_i = a_i - a_{i-1} + 0.6 \, a_{i-2}$, and fitting an MA(2) as well as the identified ARMA(1,1) gave

Model	Parameter estimates	S.E's of estimates	$\hat{\sigma}_a^2$	χ^2
ARMA(1,1)	$\hat{\phi} = -0.631$	0.073		
	$\hat{\theta} = -0.269$	0.077	0.997	49.82
MA(2)	$\hat{\theta}_1 = -1.010$	0.053		
	$\hat{\theta}_2 = 0.635$	0.054	0.864	20.98

Comment.

Solution: The two models are not very different. Rewriting the ARMA model in MA form

$$z_i = (1 + 0.631B)^{-1}(1 - 0.269B)a_i$$

$$= (1 - 0.900B + 0.568B^2 - 0.358B^3 + \ldots)a_i$$

which is significantly different from the MA(2) fit.

The shock variance is substantially smaller for the MA(2) fit, so this would be favoured, if it had not been shown inadmissible at the identification stage. However, we in fact know that the process was MA(2) and very closely approximated by the MA(2) fit. It must therefore be concluded that inadmissibility can be overruled.

If we hypothesise that ρ_1 takes its minimum value of -0.707, we have an overshoot of magnitude 0.012. Now Bartlett's formula gives

$$\text{Var}\,[r_1] > \frac{1 + 2 \times 0.7^2}{200} \simeq 0.01$$

so S.E.$[r_1] > 0.1$, and the overshoot is very insignificant. (Cf. identification of the process *5.1(b)* in exercise 7.7).

However, without knowledge of the generating process, an ARMA (1,1) model could well have been fitted and accepted, with only the diagnostic checks discussed so far (but *see Figure 9.1(a)*).

Should we have to rely on the results themselves pointing to any model inadequacy, an analysis of the shock estimates is helpful. Under the null hypothesis that the model

$$\phi(B)z_i = \theta(B)a_i \tag{9.1}$$

is of the correct form, it can be shown that the estimates

$$\hat{a}_i = \hat{\theta}^{-1}(B)\,\hat{\phi}(B)z_i$$

are related to the actual shocks by

$$\hat{a}_i = a_i + O_p \ [1/\sqrt{N}] \tag{9.2}$$

where 'O_p' denotes *order in probability*[17], and roughly means 'the order is almost certainly'.

So, as the series length increases, the behaviour of the shock estimates should approach that of a w.n. process. This can be tested by inputting them to the Program (Appendix II), and inspecting the a.c.f. and p.a.c.f. output. In particular, if the model is correct, their autocorrelations, $r_k(\hat{a})$, should be uncorrelated and for $k > 5$, say

$$r_k(\hat{a}) \approx IN(0, 1/N) \tag{9.3}$$

This result is suggested by another, due to R.L. Anderson[11], for the estimated autocorrelations of the true shocks

$$r_k(a) \approx IN(0, 1/N) \tag{9.4}$$

However, Box and Pierce[18] have shown that when the shocks are replaced by their estimates, obtained after fitting the correct form of model, this result is misleading for small k. Then the $r_k(\hat{a})$ can be highly correlated and their variances can be much lower than $1/N$.

For instance, for an AR(1) process,

$$\text{Cov} \ [r_i(\hat{a}), r_j(\hat{a})] \ \simeq \frac{1}{N} \ \{\delta_{ij} - \phi^{i+j-2} \ (1-\phi^2)\} \tag{9.5}$$

where δ_{ij} is the Kronecker delta, defined by

$$\delta_{ij} = 1 \text{ if } i = j, \ \delta_{ij} = 0 \text{ if } i \neq j$$

In particular

$$\text{Var}[r_k(\hat{a})] \simeq \frac{1}{N} \ \{1 - \phi^{2(k-1)} \ (1 - \phi^2)\} \tag{9.6}$$

So

$$\text{Var}[r_1(\hat{a})] \ \simeq \ \phi^2/N \tag{9.7}$$

though for moderate and large k

$$\text{Var}[r_k(\hat{a})] \ \simeq \ 1/N$$

and the $r_k(\hat{a})$ are uncorrelated.

How are such results derived? The general AR(p) process can be written in random shock form as $z_i = \psi(B)a_i$. If the process is stationary, $\Sigma \ \psi^2$ is finite, and the ψ weights die out quite quickly, provided the AR operator is not too close to being non-stationary, and then we can take the ψ_j's to be negligible for all $j >$ some m.

Define a p-column matrix

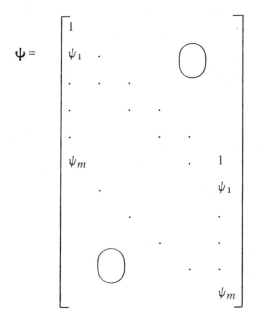

$$\psi = \begin{bmatrix} 1 & & & & & \\ \psi_1 & \cdot & & & & \\ \cdot & \cdot & \cdot & & & \\ \cdot & & \cdot & \cdot & & \\ \cdot & & & \cdot & & \\ \psi_m & & & \cdot & 1 & \\ & & & \cdot & \psi_1 & \\ & & & & \cdot & \\ & & & & \cdot & \\ & & & & \psi_m \end{bmatrix}$$

and $Q = \psi(\psi^T\psi)^{-1}\psi^T$. Then it can be shown[18] that

$$\hat{r} = [\, r_1\,(\hat{a}) \ldots r_{m+p}\,(\hat{a})\,]^T \,\dot{\sim}\, N(0, \tfrac{1}{N}[I-Q])\tag{9.8}$$

where $[I-Q]$ is idempotent and of rank m.

Exercise 9.4 Deduce the AR(1) results.

Solution: For $z_i = \phi z_{i-1} + a_i,\; -1 < \phi < 1,$

$$\psi = \begin{bmatrix} 1 \\ \psi_1 \\ \cdot \\ \cdot \\ \cdot \\ \cdot \end{bmatrix} = \begin{bmatrix} 1 \\ \phi \\ \phi^2 \\ \cdot \\ \cdot \\ \cdot \end{bmatrix}$$

so

$$Q = \begin{bmatrix} 1 \\ \phi \\ \cdot \\ \cdot \\ \cdot \end{bmatrix} (1-\phi^2) \quad [1 \ \phi \ \ldots]$$

$$= (1-\phi^2) \begin{bmatrix} 1 & \phi & \cdot & \cdot & \cdot \\ \phi & \phi^2 & \cdot & \cdot & \cdot \\ & \cdot & \cdot & \cdot & \\ & \cdot & \cdot & & \cdot \\ & \cdot & & \cdot & \end{bmatrix}$$

$$= (1-\phi^2) \Phi$$

say, where $\Phi = [\Phi_{ij}] = [\phi^{i+j-2}]$.

So

$$I - Q = [\delta_{ij} - (1-\phi^2)\phi^{i+j-2}]$$

and equation 9.8 then yields equation 9.5.

Exercise 9.5 For the AR(2) process, $z_i = \phi_1 z_{i-1} + \phi_2 z_{i-2} + a_i$ find $\text{Var}\,[r_1(\hat{a})]$, $\text{Var}[r_2(\hat{a})]$ and $\text{Cov}[r_1(\hat{a}), r_2(\hat{a})]$.

Solution:

$$\psi^T = \begin{bmatrix} 1 & \psi_1 & \cdot & \cdot & \cdot & \cdot \\ 0 & 1 & \psi_1 & \cdot & \cdot & \cdot \end{bmatrix}$$

so

$$\psi^T \psi = \begin{bmatrix} \Sigma \psi_j^2 & \Sigma \psi_{j+1}\,\psi_j \\ \Sigma \psi_{j+1}\,\psi_j & \Sigma \psi_j^2 \end{bmatrix}$$

$$= \frac{\sigma_z^2}{\sigma_a^2} \begin{bmatrix} 1 & \rho_1 \\ \rho_1 & 1 \end{bmatrix}$$

So

$$Q = \frac{\sigma_a^2/\sigma_z^2}{(1-\rho_1^2)} \begin{bmatrix} 1 & 0 \\ \psi_1 & 1 \\ & \psi_1 \\ . & . \\ . & . \\ . & . \end{bmatrix} \begin{bmatrix} 1 & -\rho_1 \\ -\rho_1 & 1 \end{bmatrix} \begin{bmatrix} 1 & \psi_1 & . & . & . & . \\ 0 & 1 & \psi_1 & . & . & . \end{bmatrix}$$

$$= \frac{\sigma_a^2/\sigma_z^2}{(1-\rho_1^2)} \begin{bmatrix} 1 & -\rho_1 \\ \psi_1 - \rho_1 & -\psi_1\rho_1 + 1 \\ . & . \\ . & . \\ . & . \end{bmatrix} \begin{bmatrix} 1 & \psi_1 & . & . & . & . \\ 0 & 1 & \psi_1 & . & . & . \end{bmatrix}$$

$$= \frac{\sigma_a^2/\sigma_z^2}{(1-\rho_1^2)} \begin{bmatrix} 1 & \psi_1 - \rho_1 & . & . & . & . \\ . & (\psi_1 - \rho_1)\psi_1 - \psi_1\rho_1 + 1 & . & . & . & . \\ . & . & . & & & \\ . & . & & . & & \\ . & . & & & . & \\ . & . & & & & . \end{bmatrix}$$

Now $\psi_1 = \phi_1, \rho_1 = \phi_1/(1-\phi_2)$ and

$$\sigma_a^2/\sigma_z^2 = (1+\phi_2)\{(1-\phi_2)^2 - \phi_1^2\}/(1-\phi_2)$$

so

$$Q = (1 - \phi_2^2) \begin{bmatrix} 1 & -\phi_1 \phi_2/(1 - \phi_2) & \cdot & \cdot & \cdot & \cdot \\ \cdot & \{1 - \phi_2 - \phi_1^2 \, (1 + \phi_2)\}/(1 - \phi_2) & \cdot & \cdot & \cdot & \cdot \\ \cdot & & & & & \\ \cdot & & \cdot & & & \\ \cdot & & \cdot & & & \\ \cdot & & \cdot & & & \cdot \end{bmatrix}$$

and

$$I-Q = \begin{bmatrix} \phi_2^2 & \phi_1 \phi_2 \, (1 + \phi_2) & \cdot & \cdot & \cdot & \cdot \\ \cdot & \phi_2^2 + \phi_1^2 \, (1 + \phi_2)^2 & \cdot & \cdot & \cdot & \cdot \\ \cdot & & & & & \\ \cdot & & \cdot & & & \\ \cdot & & \cdot & & & \\ \cdot & & \cdot & & & \end{bmatrix}$$

Thus, using equation 9.8, for an AR(2) process

$$\left. \begin{aligned} \mathrm{Var}[r_1(\hat{a})] &\simeq \phi_2^2/N \\ \mathrm{Var}[r_2(\hat{a})] &\simeq \{\phi_2^2 + \phi_1^2 \, (1 + \phi_2)^2\}/N \\ \mathrm{Cov}[r_1(\hat{a}), r_2(\hat{a})] &\simeq \phi_1 \phi_2 \, (1 + \phi_2)/N \end{aligned} \right\} \qquad (9.9)$$

Box and Pierce[18] show that the shock estimates for an ARMA(p,q) process are close to those for an associated AR$(p+q)$ process. This of course includes MA processes as special cases with $p = 0$.
Given any ARMA(p,q) process

$$\phi(B)z_i = \theta(B)a_i$$

and the particular related AR$(p + q)$ process

$$\phi(B) \, \theta(B)z_i = a_i$$

then, if series realisations for these two processes are generated from the same set of shocks $\{a_i\}$, the shock estimates after efficiently fitting both series are roughly the same.

Thus the distribution of $\{r_k(\hat{a})\}$ for any ARMA(p,q) series can be approximately obtained by considering equation 9.8 for the related AR($p+q$) series, though naturally this requires correct identification of p and q.

Exercise 9.6   When an AR(1) fit was efficiently estimated for the series of exercise 7.3, the following results were obtained.

$$\hat{\phi} = -0{\cdot}805, r_1(\hat{a}) = 0{\cdot}072, r_2(\hat{a}) = 0{\cdot}111, r_3(\hat{a}) = -0{\cdot}009$$

and all of $r_4(\hat{a})$ to $r_{20}(\hat{a})$ are smaller in magnitude than $0{\cdot}135$. What can be concluded?

Solution: From equation 9.7,

$$\mathrm{Var}[r_1(\hat{a})] \simeq \frac{0{\cdot}805^2}{200}, \text{ so S.E.}[r_1(\hat{a})] \simeq 0{\cdot}057.$$

From equation 9.6,

$$\mathrm{Var}[r_4(\hat{a})] \simeq \frac{1 - 0{\cdot}805^6 \, (1 - 0{\cdot}805^2)}{200}, \text{ so S.E.}[r_4(\hat{a})] \simeq {\cdot}0{\cdot}067.$$

Thus none of the observed $r_k(\hat{a})$ are more than twice their standard errors away from zero, and the AR(1) fit seems satisfactory.

Exercise 9.7   For series G, of exercises 7.8, 8.3 and 9.2, investigate the $\{r_k(\hat{a})\}$ for the efficient MA(1) fit.

Solution: From exercise 8.3, $\hat{\theta} = -0{\cdot}465$. Also $r_1(\hat{a}) = -0{\cdot}12, r_2(\hat{a}) = 0{\cdot}02$ and all of $r_3(\hat{a})$ to $r_{20}(\hat{a}) < 0{\cdot}19$ in magnitude.

If the MA(1) was correctly identified, the shock estimates behave roughly as those for the associated AR(1) process, $z_i = 0{\cdot}465 \, z_{i-1} + a_i$.

So $\mathrm{Var}[r_1(\hat{a})] \simeq \dfrac{0{\cdot}465^2}{100}$ and S.E.$[r_1(\hat{a})] \simeq 0{\cdot}047$. Thus the observed $r_1(\hat{a})$ is significant at about the 1% level.

$$\mathrm{Var}[r_3(\hat{a})] \simeq \frac{1 - 0{\cdot}465^4 \, (1 - 0{\cdot}465^2)}{100}, \text{ so S.E.}[r_3(\hat{a})] \simeq 0{\cdot}099, \text{ and}$$

none of the other $r_k(\hat{a})$ are significant.

There is thus an indication that the shocks are not white noise, as they should be for a correct fit, but themselves follow an MA(1) process.

Note that without the Box–Pierce results, the $r_1(\hat{a})$ would not have been suspect, and a white noise process for the shocks would have been accepted.

An easy but low powered check is the *portmanteau* lack-of-fit test[18]. This can not give much support to the model, should it prove not significant, but is easy to include in the estimation program. The statistic

$$R = N \sum_1^K r_k^2(\hat{a}) \qquad (9.10)$$

is calculated, where K is say 20. Then R contains information on the first 20 $\rho_k(\hat{a})$ taken as a whole. Should the fitted model be appropriate,

$$R \; \dot{\sim} \; \chi^2{}_{K-p-q} \qquad (9.11)$$

and a significant R indicates model inadequacy.

Equation 9.11 is slightly different from the χ_K^2 suggested by using equation 9.4 in 9.10. For an AR(p) process, using equation 9.8,

$$N \hat{r}^T \hat{r} = N \sum_1^{m+p} r_k^2(\hat{a}) \; \dot{\sim} \; \chi_m^2$$

It is apparent that if we extend $\boldsymbol{\psi}$, by replacing m by $M > m$, the size of Q increases but its rank remains the same and

$$N \sum_1^{M+p} r_k^2(\hat{a}) \; \dot{\sim} \; \chi_M^2$$

So, choosing $K \gg m + p$,

$$N \sum_1^K r_k^2(\hat{a}) \; \dot{\sim} \; \chi^2{}_{K-p}$$

Thus, for a general ARMA(p,q) process, equation 9.11 holds, provided K is sufficiently large so that $K \gg m + p + q$, where m depends on the associated AR($p+q$) process.

For convenience, *Table 9.1* is included. It is intended that K should each time be chosen to give $K - p - q = 20$.

Table 9.1 $(100 - \alpha)\%$ significance points for χ_{20}^2

α	10	5	1	0.1
Critical point	28.41	31.41	37.57	45.31

For example, in exercise 9.1, the χ^2 for the identified MA(1) was not significant. The same is true for exercise 9.2. In exercise 9.3, the (incorrectly) identified ARMA(1,1) fit would have been rejected owing to a very highly significant χ^2 value, while the χ^2 for the correct MA(2) fit was not significant.

Exercise 9.8 Fitting various models to the series of exercise 7.6, which was generated by an AR(2) process, gave

Model	Parameter estimates	S.E's of estimates	$\hat{\sigma}_a^2$	χ^2
AR(1)	$\hat{\phi} = 0.429$	0.065	0.926	64.18
ARMA(1,1)	$\hat{\phi} = 0.781$	0.071		
	$\hat{\theta} = -0.424$	0.111	0.861	36.59
AR(2)	$\hat{\phi}_1 = 0.285$	0.067		
	$\hat{\phi}_2 = 0.360$	0.067	0.805	18.43
AR(3)	$\hat{\phi}_1 = 0.348$	0.072		
	$\hat{\phi}_2 = 0.405$	0.070		
	$\hat{\phi}_3 = -0.168$	0.071	0.785	12.89

Comment.

Solution: The χ^2 value for the AR(1) fit is very highly significant. It is approaching high significance for the ARMA(1,1) overfit, while for the AR(2) overfit, it is not significant. In fact an AR(2) was identified, with some evidence of an AR(3), which also, not unexpectedly, gives a non-significant χ^2.

Thus the underfitted AR(1) and the incorrect ARMA(1,1) are both unacceptable, as was seen at the identification stage. But a decision on which of the higher order AR to accept requires further consideration.

The shock variance for the AR(3) is not very much smaller, nor are the parameters $\hat{\phi}_1$ and $\hat{\phi}_2$ significantly different from the corresponding estimates for the AR(2). However, $\hat{\phi}_3$ is significantly different from zero, as was suspected at the identification stage, so we conclude that the AR(3) overfit is justified. An incorrect conclusion, as we know, but supported by the evidence.

Suppose the $\hat{a}_i$ obtained from fitting model 9.1 appear not to be close to white noise. Then the $\{r_k(\hat{a})\}$ and $\{\hat{\phi}_{kk}(\hat{a})\}$ may suggest a model for the series $\{a_i\}$

$$\phi^*(B)a_i = \theta^*(B)b_i \qquad (9.12)$$

where $\{b_i\}$ is a w.n. process. Then, eliminating a_i from model 9.1 and 9.12 gives

$$\phi^*(B)\phi(B)z_i = \theta^*(B)\theta(B)b_i$$

an ARMA($p + p^*, q + q^*$) model. The ϕ and θ parameters will have been obtained in estimating the identified model 9.1, whilst the ϕ^*'s and θ^*'s are obtained from estimating model 9.12.

Exercise 9.9 In exercise 9.7, there was evidence that the shocks, after fitting $z_i = a_i - 0\cdot465\, a_{i-1}$ to series G, themselves followed on MA(1) process. Investigate this further, and if necessary modify the fit.

Solution:
$$\hat{\theta}_0^* = \frac{1 - \sqrt{(1 - 4 \times 0\cdot1214^2)}}{2 \times -0\cdot1214} = -0\cdot12$$

Efficient estimation then gives $\hat{\theta}^* = -0\cdot054$, S.E.$[\hat{\theta}^*] = 0\cdot100$, so $\hat{\theta}^*$ is not significant. This suggests that any departures of the shocks from white noise are not really important. This conclusion is supported by the fact that, on combining the MA fits for G and its shock estimates series, a model $z_i = b_i - 0\cdot519\, b_{i-1} + 0\cdot025\, b_{i-2}$ is obtained. The second parameter is nowhere near significant (from *Table 8.1*:

$\text{Var}[\hat{\theta}_2] \simeq \dfrac{1 - 0\cdot025^2}{100}$), and an MA(2) overfit to G has already been

rejected in exercise 9.2. Thus the original fit to G is retained.

In the author's opinion, the Box—Pierce results, though interesting theoretically, are, as in this case, of limited use in practice. For, if the early $r_k(\hat{a})$ are so small that their significance can only be picked up by the Box—Pierce formulae, then the shock series, for practical purposes, is indistinguishable from white noise.

In general, when model building, the time series analyst must always consider whether a fit, statistically inadequate, is in practical terms adequate. As an analogy, a draughtsman would not discard a straight edge just because it was shown jagged under a microscope.

Finally, we consider the *cumulative periodogram* check on the shock estimates. The theory for this belongs to the 'frequency domain' which we are not considering in this book[1], so we will just give the results.

Define the *periodogram* for the series $\hat{a}_1, \ldots, \hat{a}_N$ by

$$I(r) = \frac{2}{N} \left(\sum_{i=1}^{N} \hat{a}_i \cos 2\pi \frac{r}{N} i \right)^2 + \left(\sum_{i=1}^{N} \hat{a}_i \sin 2\pi \frac{r}{N} i \right)^2$$

for $r = 1, \ldots, \left[\frac{N-2}{2}\right]$, where [ ] denotes the 'integer part of'. Then the *(standardised) cumulative periodogram* is defined by

$$C(j) = \frac{\sum_{r=1}^{j} I(r)}{N\hat{\sigma}_a^2} \quad \text{for } j = 1, \ldots, \left[\frac{N-2}{2}\right]$$

$$C\left(\left[N/2\right]\right) = 1$$

We plot $C(j)$ against j/N, and if the series comes from a white noise process, the plot will be scattered randomly about the join of (0,0) to (0·5, 1). Inadequacies in the fit show up as systematic deviations from this line, and the significance of such deviations is assessed by the *Kolmogorov–Smirnov* test[19].

For our purposes, the mechanics of this test are:

1. Obtain D, the maximum vertical deviation of the plot from the white noise join.
2. Compare D with its critical points, which, for $M = \left[\frac{N-1}{2}\right] > 35$, are given in *Table 9.2*.

Table 9.2 Two-tailed $(100 - \alpha)\%$ critical points, k_α, for D

α	10	5	1
$\sqrt{(M)}k_\alpha$	1·22	1·36	1·63

Usually the results are presented by superimposing parallel dotted lines k_α above and below the white noise join. If the plot crosses either of these critical lines, the result is significant at the $\alpha\%$ level. The causes of significant values will be both model inadequacy and fitting error (and, of course, chance).

An example of an inadequate fit spotlighted by this test is given in

Figure 9.1(a). However, the test is not very sensitive and, for non-seasonal series, rarely spots inadequacies, which the other tests have missed, if the identification and estimation have been sensibly carried out.

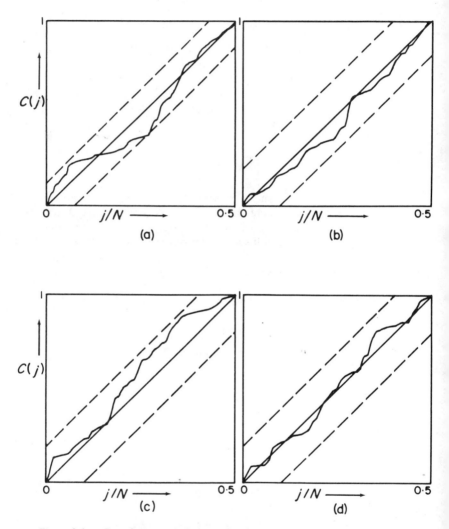

Figure 9.1   Cumulative periodograms for shock estimates after fitting
(a) ARMA(1,1) in exercise 9.3; (b) MA(1) to series G;
(c) AR(2) to series K; (d) AR(3) to series K
(dotted lines give 95% C.I's for white noise process of same length)

Exercise 9.10 Write a program for the cumulative periodogram check, and run it with the shock estimates from the MA(1) fit to series G. Comment.

Solution: The results are given in *Figure 9.1(b)*, and no inadequacy of fit is detected.

Exercise 9.11 Either use your program, or a Box–Jenkins pack, to run the shock estimates from the AR(2) fit to series K through the cumulative periodogram check.

Solution: *Figure 9.1(c)* does not indicate a significant lack of fit.

However, there are indications from previous results that an AR(2) fit might be inadequate. For instance $r_9(\hat{a})$ is significant, and using the Box–Pierce results, so is r_1 $(\hat{a})$. Also when Box and Jenkins[2] identified the process, ϕ_{33} proved significant, though the author did not find this to be the case.

Exercise 9.12 Overfit an AR(3) model, and apply diagnostic checks.

Solution: Efficient estimation gives

$$z_i = 11{\cdot}59 + 1{\cdot}56 z_{i-1} - 1{\cdot}02 z_{i-2} + 0{\cdot}21 z_{i-3} + a_i$$

with S.E.$[\hat{\phi}_{33}] = 0{\cdot}10$. So $\hat{\phi}_3$ is significant. $\hat{\sigma}_a^2 = 219{\cdot}4$, which seems a slight improvement on $227{\cdot}5$. The fit does not appear good at the beginning of the series, where the 3rd, 5th, 7th and 14th shock estimates are significant, but only one other is. The χ^2 is reduced from $23{\cdot}94$ to $17{\cdot}81$, which seems to be better, but $r_9(\hat{a})$ is still significant. The cumulative periodogram for the shock estimates is given in *Figure 9.1(d)* and appears to be an improvement. A reasonable conclusion is that the AR(3) fit is preferable.

However, the persistence of a significant $r_9(\hat{a})$ suggests something is still wrong, and this is supported by the continued significance of $\hat{\phi}_{11,11}(\hat{a})$ if the estimated shock p.a.c.f's are also investigated.

Should a fit stand up to diagnostic checks it is not proved correct, just shown to be plausible, and is adequate only in this sense. In some cases it is to be hoped that a satisfactorily fitted model may throw some light on the mechanism at work.

In Chapters 11 and 12 there will be a chance to *verify* models fitted to further real occurring series, and we will revert there to the term 'residual' for shock estimate.

10

Forecasting

Consider a stationary series $\{z_i\}$ arising from an **ARMA** process. Let $\hat{z}_i(l)$ be the *forecast* of z_{i+l} made at the time i. Then $\hat{z}_i(l)$, $l = 1, 2, \ldots$ is called the *forecast function* at i for *lead l*. If the length of the observed series to date is large, the estimation errors in the parameters will generally not be serious, and so, assuming the model to be known exactly for the past and to *remain unchanged in the future,* minimum mean square error forecasts may be obtained as follows.

Suppose the best possible forecast, linear in current and previous a_i, is given by

$$\hat{z}_i(l) = \psi_l{}^*a_i + \psi_{l+1}{}^* a_{i-1} + \ldots$$

where the ψ^* weights are to be determined. The random shock form of the **ARMA** model is

$$z_{i+l} = (a_{i+l} + \psi_1 a_{i+l-1} + \ldots + \psi_{l-1} a_{i+1}) + (\psi_l a_i + \ldots$$

so

$$E[\{z_{i+l}-\hat{z}_i(l)\}^2] = (1+\psi_1^2 + \ldots + \psi^2{}_{l-1})\sigma_a^2 + \sum_{j=l}^{\infty} (\psi_j-\psi_j{}^*)^2 \; \sigma_a^2$$

and this is plainly a minimum when

$$\psi_j^* = \psi_j \quad j = l, l+1, \ldots$$

So

$$\hat{z}_i(l) = \psi_l a_i + \psi_{l+1} a_{i-1} + \ldots \tag{10.1}$$

The *forecast error* at i for lead l is

$$e_i(l) = z_{i+l} - \hat{z}_i(l) = a_{i+l} + \psi_1 a_{i+l-1} + \ldots + \psi_{l-1} a_{i+1} \tag{10.2}$$

Let $E\limits_{i}$, the *conditional expectation operator,* denote 'the expected value at time i of '. Then

$$E\limits_{i} [a_{i+l}] \neq 0, \qquad l > 0$$

$$= a_{i+l}, \qquad l \leqslant 0$$

So equation 10.1 gives

$$E\limits_{i} [\hat{z}_i(l)] = \hat{z}_i(l), \quad l > 0$$

and equation 10.2 yields

$$E\limits_{i} [e_i(l)] = 0, \qquad l > 0 \qquad\qquad (10.3)$$

$$E\limits_{i} [z_{i+l}] = \hat{z}_i(l), \quad l > 0 \qquad\qquad (10.4)$$

Also clearly

$$E\limits_{i} [z_{i+l}] = z_{i+l}, \quad l < 0$$

Equation 10.3 shows that the forecast error has zero expected value, and equation 10.4 that the forecasts are unbiased.

However, should the forecast function for any series wander off target to either side, it is likely to remain there in the short run at any rate, and the forecast errors at various leads will be correlated.

Exercise 10.1   Prove this last point.

Solution: From equation 10.2

$$e_i(l) = \sum_{j=0}^{l-1} \psi_j\, a_{i+l-j}$$

and for m > 0

$$e_i(l + m) = \sum_{j=0}^{l+m-1} \psi_j a_{i+l+m-j}$$

Also

$$E[e_i(l)] = E[e_i(l+m)] = 0$$

so

$$\text{Cov}\,[e_i(l), e_i(l+m)] = \sum_{j=0}^{l-1} \psi_j \psi_{j+m}\, \sigma_a^2$$

In general this is not zero and the correlation will depend on both l and m.

The one step ahead forecast errors are in fact the shocks which generate the process, and so of course are uncorrelated. This is seen by putting $l = 1$ in equation 10.2. However, for various forecast origins, the forecast errors for a particular lead time will often be correlated.

Exercise 10.2   Prove this last point.

Solution: From equation 10.2

$$e_i(l) = \sum_{j=0}^{l-1} \psi_j\, a_{i+l-j}$$

$$e_{i+m}(l) = \sum_{j=0}^{l-1} \psi_j\, a_{i+m+l-j}$$

So if $|m| \geqslant l$,

$$\text{Cov}\,[e_i(l), e_{i+m}(l)] = 0$$

but if $|m| < l$,

$$\text{Cov}\,[e_i(l), e_{i+m}(l)] = \sum_{j=0}^{l-1-|m|} \psi_j\, \psi_{j+|m|}\, \sigma_a^2$$

which is not in general zero.

From equation 10.2, the variance of the forecast error at lead l is given by

$$V(l) = \text{Var}\,[e_i(l)] = (1 + \psi_1^2 + \ldots + \psi_{l-1}^2)\, \sigma_a^2 \qquad (10.5)$$

which remains finite for all stationary processes, being $\leqslant \sigma_z^2$, and hence $(100-\alpha)\%$ confidence intervals for the forecasts are obtained as

$$\hat{z}_i(l) \pm k_\alpha \left\{ \left(\sum_{j=0}^{l-1} \psi_j^2 \right) \sigma_a^2 \right\}^{\frac{1}{2}}$$

where k_α is the $(100-\alpha/2)\%$ point of the standardised normal distribution. For series of length $N > 50$, such as we are considering, we can replace σ_a^2 by its efficient estimate, the critical points of the relevant student's 't' being very close to those of the normal.

Since the forecasts are unbiased and have minimum mean square error, they have minimum variance in the linear class.

The difference equation form of an ARMA(p,q) process is

$$z_{i+l} = \phi_1 z_{i+l-1} + \ldots + \phi_p z_{i+l-p} + a_{i+l} + \theta_1 a_{i+l-1} + \ldots + \theta_q a_{i+l-q}$$

So, taking conditional expectations at time i, for $l > 0$ the optimal forecast function can be written as

$$\hat{z}_i(l) = \phi_1 \, \underset{i}{E} \, [z_{i+l-1}] + \ldots + \phi_p \, \underset{i}{E} \, [z_{i+l-p}]$$

$$+ 0 + \theta_1 \, \underset{i}{E} \, [a_{i+l-1}] + \ldots + \theta_q \, \underset{i}{E} \, [a_{i+l-q}] \qquad (10.6)$$

Thus for $1 < l < p$, q say,

$$\hat{z}_i(l) = \phi_1 \, \hat{z}_i(l-1) + \ldots + \phi_{l-1} \hat{z}_i(1) + \phi_l z_i + \ldots + \phi_p z_{i+l-p}$$

$$+ \theta_l a_i + \ldots + \theta_q a_{i+l-q}$$

Equation 10.6 is the most convenient form to use in practice.

Starting with an observed series of length N for which forecasts are required for leads up to L, we calculate the $\hat{z}_N(l)$, $l = 1, \ldots, L$ recursively to fill up line (A) of *Table 10.1*, where if necessary some initial unknown a's may need to be set to zero.

When z_{N+1} becomes available we obtain, using equation 10.2,

$$a_{N+1} = z_{N+1} - \hat{z}_N(1) \qquad (10.7)$$

and then can easily update the forecasts for leads $1, \ldots, L-1$, by writing

$$\hat{z}_{N+1}(l) = \hat{z}_N(l+1) + \psi_l a_{N+1} \qquad (10.8)$$

Table 10.1

i	z_i	a_i	lead l					
			1	2	$\ldots$	$L-1$	L	.
N	z_N		$\hat{z}_N(1)$	$\hat{z}_N(2)$	$\ldots$	$\hat{z}_N(L-1)$	$\hat{z}_N(L)$	(A)
$N+1$	z_{N+1}	a_{N+1}	$\hat{z}_{N+1}(1)$	$\hat{z}_{N+1}(2)$	$\ldots$	$\hat{z}_{N+1}(L-1)$	$\hat{z}_{N+1}(L)$	(B)
$(100-\alpha)\%$ Confidence Limits $\pm$			λ_1	λ_2	$\ldots$	λ_{L-1}	λ_L	(Z)

$$\text{where } \lambda_l = k_\alpha \left\{ \left(\sum_0^{l-1} \psi_j^2 \right) \sigma_a^2 \right\}^{\frac{1}{2}}, \quad l = 1, \ldots L.$$

This follows since equation 10.1 yields

$$\hat{z}_{N+1}(l) = \psi_l a_{N+1} + \psi_{l+1} a_N + \psi_{l+2} a_{N-1} + \ldots$$

and

$$\hat{z}_N(l+1) = \psi_{l+1} a_N + \psi_{l+2} a_{N-1} + \ldots$$

which on subtraction gives equation 10.8. Since we do not have $\hat{z}_N(L + 1)$, we can only proceed up to $\hat{z}_{N+1}(L-1)$. However $\hat{z}_{N+1}(L)$ is easily found then on re-applying equation 10.6. Line (B) of *Table 10.1* is thus obtained, and so on indefinitely. It is convenient to include the confidence limits, for the various leads, as line (Z) of *Table 10.1*. These limits apply to the *individual* forecasts for z_{i+l}, conditional on the information available at the origin i.

Exercise 10.3 Use the first 97 values of series G (Appendix I) to forecast for leads up to 3, giving 95% confidence limits, and then update these forecasts, by taking account of the 98th value.

Solution: Strictly speaking, it is incorrect to use the model, fitted to the whole series, to forecast the last part of it. Evidently this procedure, for testing a forecasting method, would give misleadingly good results, since any vagaries of the values to be forecast will have already modified the fit. However, since here we do have nearly the complete series, we will not bother to refit the truncated series.

For the MA(1) fit equation 10.6 gives

$$\hat{z}_{97}(1) = -0.465 \times -0.9406 = 0.4374$$

and

$$\hat{z}_{97}(2) = \hat{z}_{97}(3) = 0$$

Note that the 97th shock estimate, obtained from the output of exercise 8.3, has been used for the corresponding shock.

$$\lambda_1 \simeq 2\sqrt{(1 \times 0.872)} = 1.9$$

$$\lambda_2 \simeq 2\sqrt{\{(1 + 0.465^2) \times 0.872\}} = 2.1$$

so C.I's for z_{98} and z_{99} are, respectively, $(-1.5, 2.3)$ and $(-2.1, 2.1)$.

Then, when the 98th value comes available, from equation 10.7

$$a_{98} = 0.49 - 0.4374 = 0.0526$$

so equation 10.8 gives

$$\hat{z}_{98}(1) = 0 - 0 - 0.465 \times 0.0526 = -0.0245$$

while from equation 10.6

$$\hat{z}_{98}(2) = 0$$

Exercise 10.4 Obtain forecasts for the next 20 values of the Wölfer sunspot numbers by (a) visual extrapolation and (b) using the AR(3) fit obtained in exercise 9.12.

Solution: The forecasts are shown in *Figure 10.1*.

Both have underestimated the first peak, but apart from this, the extrapolated forecast is far better. In particular, the damping to the mean for the AR(3) forecast does not appear very realistic, given the series to date. In general, when the model is not adequate, visual extrapolation is probably the best method of forecasting, using just the information contained in the series history. (If other information is available, the extrapolation can be modified).

Note that poor forecasting performance can indicate model inadequacy. Granger[20] even suggests using the discrepancies between forecasts and the future values, when they come available, as a diagnostic check, which could show how a model needs modifying. The possibilities of this have not yet been tested in practice.

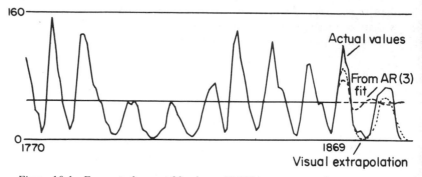

Figure 10.1   Forecasts for next 20 values of Wölfer sunspot numbers

Exercise 10.5   Show that there is unlikely to be much difference between the one step ahead forecasts obtained using the estimated and correct models for series G.

Solution: Denote the forecasts from the correct and estimated models by $\check{z}_i(l)$ and $\hat{z}_i(l)$, respectively, and the mistaken shock values when using the estimated model in equation 10.7 by $\check{a}_i$. Then

$$\check{z}_i(1) = -0.465\, \check{a}_i$$

$$\hat{z}_i(1) = -0.6\, a_i$$

$$\check{z}_i(l) = \hat{z}_i(l) = 0, \; l > 1$$

So, for leads greater than 1, there is no difference in forecasts, and writing Δ for the difference, $\check{z}_i(1) - \hat{z}_i(1)$,

$$\Delta = 0.6\, a_i - 0.465\, \check{a}_i \tag{10.9}$$

Now

$$z_{i+1} = (1 - 0.465B)\, \check{a}_i = (1 - 0.6B)\, a_i$$

so

$$\check{a}_i = \left(\frac{1 - 0.6B}{1 - 0.465B} \right) a_i$$

and equation 10.9 becomes

$$\Delta = \frac{0.135}{1 - 0.465B}\, a_i$$

So

$$E[\Delta] = 0$$

and

$$\text{Var}[\Delta] = \frac{0.135^2}{1 - 0.465^2} \, \sigma_a^2$$

$$= 0.02325 \, \sigma_a^2$$

Thus $\text{Var}[\Delta]$ is small compared with $\text{Var}[\hat{z}_i(1)] = 0.36 \, \sigma_a^2$, and assuming Δ is roughly normally distributed, $\tilde{z}_i(1)$ is within $\pm 2\sqrt{(0.02325 \times 1)} = \pm 0.31$ of $\hat{z}_i(1)$, with 95% certainty.

We will conclude this chapter with a useful method for determining the shape of forecast functions. For time $i + l$, the ARMA(p,q) model gives

$$\phi(B)z_{i+l} = \theta(B)a_{i+l}$$

So, taking conditional expectations and using equation 10.6, for $l > q$

$$\phi(B)\hat{z}_i(l) = 0$$

a difference equation which is solved in terms of the p starting, or pivotal, values $\hat{z}_i(q-p+1), \ldots, \hat{z}_i(q)$ where $\hat{z}_i(j) = z_{i+j}$ for $j \leqslant 0$. So at leads $> q-p$, the $\hat{z}_i(l)$ follow a function, called the eventual forecast function, abbreviated to e.f.f., whose form is dependent on the AR operator. The e.f.f. is simple to determine in any particular case using the pivotal values, which are related to recent values of the process through the MA operator.

Exercise 10.6 Find the form of the e.f.f. for the ARMA$(1,2)$ process.

Solution: For $l > 2$, $(1 - \phi B)\hat{z}_i(l) = 0$, so $\hat{z}_i(l) = A\phi^l$, where A is obtained from the single pivotal value $\hat{z}_i(2) = A\phi^2$. So the e.f.f. is fully determined by the forecast at lead 2, and decays geometrically from this forecast. $\hat{z}_i(2)$ can be obtained from

$$\hat{z}_i(2) = \phi\hat{z}_i(1) + \theta_2 a_i$$

and

$$\hat{z}_i(1) = \phi z_i + \theta_1 a_i + \theta_2 a_{i-1}$$

where, in practice, the shocks have to be replaced by their estimates.

Exercise 10.7 Plot the ARMA$(1,2)$ e.f.f. when

$$\phi = 0.5, \ \theta_1 = -0.8, \theta_2 = 0.4,$$

$$z_i = 3.24, \ a_i = 0.64 \text{ and } a_{i-1} = 0.95$$

Solution:

$$\hat{z}_i(1) = 1 \cdot 62 - 0 \cdot 512 + 0 \cdot 38 = 1 \cdot 488$$

$$\hat{z}_i(2) = 0 \cdot 744 + 0 \cdot 256 = 1 \cdot 000$$

So $A = 4$, and the plot is given in *Figure 10.2*.

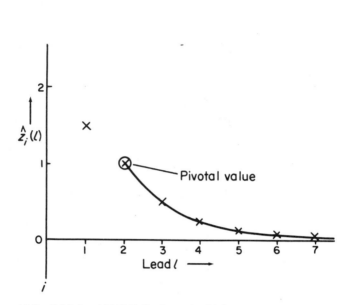

Figure 10.2 E.f.f. for ARMA(1,2) of exercise 10.7

The Box—Jenkins forecasts are *robust* to errors in the parameter estimates. That is to say, not much precision is lost by replacing the parameters by their efficient estimates in the forecast function. An example of this has already been investigated in exercise 10.5. For a series of moderate length N, it would seem that the increase in the C.I. of a forecast, resulting from the parameters being estimated, is often only of order $1/N$. This insensitivity of the forecasts to estimation errors is fortunate for practical purposes.

The evidence is that for many series encountered in practice, provided some success can be achieved with building the model, Box—Jenkins forecasts are among the best, and often the best, for short leads, provided the series to date is not too short ($N > 50$ say for non-seasonal series)[9,52].

11

Integrated Processes

Many observed non-stationary time series exhibit a certain homogeneity and can be accounted for by a simple modification of the ARMA model, the *autoregressive integrated moving average* model. This ARIMA (p,d,q) model is written

$$\varphi(B)z_i = \theta(B)a_i \qquad (11.1)$$

where $\varphi(B)$, the *generalised autoregressive operator*, is a polynomial of degree $p + d$ with exactly d zeros equal to unity, and all the others outside the unit circle. So

$$\varphi(B) = \phi_p(B)(1-B)^d = \phi_p(B)\nabla^d$$

where $\phi_p(B)$ is a *stationary autoregressive operator* of order p.

If we replace $\nabla^d z_i$ by w_i, the ARIMA(p,d,q) process for $\{z_i\}$ is reduced to an ARMA(p,q) process for $\{w_i\}$, and the theory of the previous chapters applies. Should there be evidence that $E[w_i] \neq 0$, $\widetilde{w}_i = w_i - \overline{w}$ is used instead. Having found the $\{w_i\}$ process, the $\{z_i\}$ process can be obtained by the operation inverse to the differencing ∇^d, that is by summing or *integrating* the stationary $\{w_i\}$ process d times.

For instance, consider a process which would be stationary except that it has randomly occurring shifts in *level*. We require a model whose behaviour is not influenced by the current level of the process, such that given any constant M

$$\varphi(B)(z_i + M) = \varphi(B)z_i$$

i.e.

$$\varphi(B)M = 0$$

This implies that $\varphi(1) = 0$, so $\varphi(B)$ has a factor $(1-B)$, and, if it has only one such factor, differencing once will produce a stationary series.

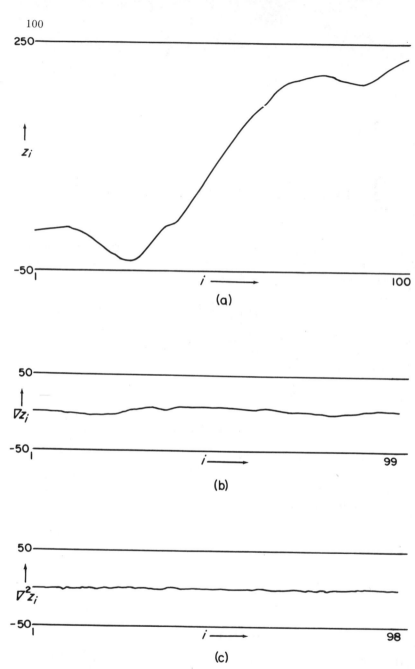

(a)

(b)

(c)

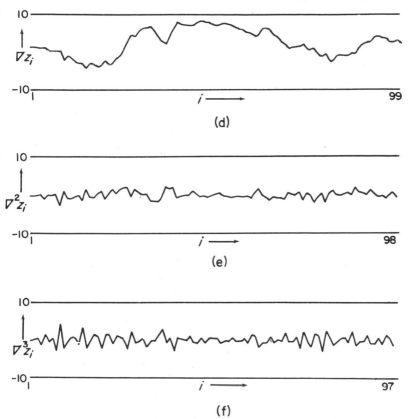

Figure 11.1 Simulated series $(1\text{-}B)^2 z_i = a_i$ with 1st, 2nd and 3rd differenced series

Should there also occur random shifts of *slope,* we need $\varphi(B)$ to have a factor $(1-B)^2$, and a second differencing is required to produce stationarity, and so on should stochastic *trends* of higher order exist, though in practice it is found seldom necessary to difference more than twice. We will restrict ourselves to ARIMA models with $d \leqslant 2$, and as before $p + q \leqslant 2$.

Figure 11.1 shows a simulated series $(1-B)^2 z_i = a_i$ and its first two differenced series. (a), (b) and (c) are to the same scale, and the last two of these magnified 5 times give (d) and (e). (f) shows the third differences, again magnified 5 times.

In practice, a realisation smooth like (a) indicates a generating mechanism with a large degree of inertia. The series has a varying slope,

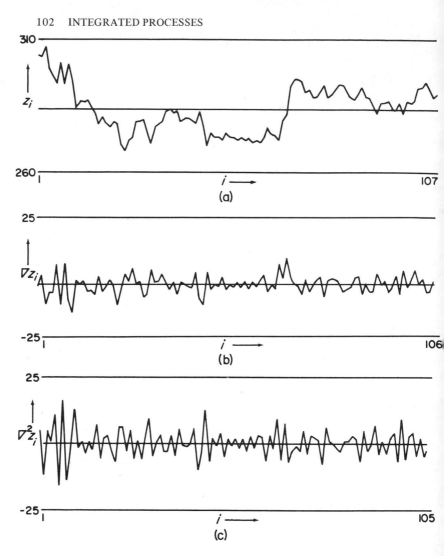

Figure 11.2   Series D*, ICI closing stock prices, with 1st and 2nd differenced series

while its first differences have no fixed level. However the second differences look stationary, as indeed they should do, being in fact simulated white noise. Also, evidently the series variance decreases with differencing until stationarity is achieved, and then increases again with *overdifferencing (f). See Table 11.1* (p. 117).

Series D* is shown in *Figure 11.2(a)* and exhibits a varying level. The differenced series (*b*) however looks stationary, while the second differences (*c*) appear to be overdifferenced.

As indicated by these two examples, the general procedure for such homogeneous non-stationarity is first to recognise it by visual inspection of the plotted series, and then to remove it by the necessary degree of differencing.

Another means of identifying it, is to consider the a.c.f. Multiplying equation 11.1 by z_{i-k} and taking expectations gives, for $k > q$,

$$\varphi(B)\rho_k = 0$$

with solution, for $k > q - p - d$,

$$\rho_k = A_1 + kA_2 + \ldots + k^{d-1}A_d + A_{d+1}\lambda_{d+1}{}^k + \ldots + A_{d+p}\lambda_{d+p}{}^k$$

$$(11.2)$$

where $\lambda_{d+1}, \ldots, \lambda_{d+p}$ (assumed distinct) all have modulus < 1. Since $|\rho_k|$ must never exceed unity, considering $k \to \infty$ gives $A_2 = \ldots = A_d = 0$ and $\rho_k \to A_1$. So the a.c.f. tends to a constant. In particular for

$$\nabla^d z_i = a_i \qquad (11.3)$$

$$\rho_k = 1 \text{ for all } k$$

In practice, for series of finite length, it is impossible to decide whether any of the AR zeros are exactly unity. However, stationary series with an AR zero approaching 1 have a wandering level and are best differenced, thus considerably reducing their variance. Such series will be called *unstable*. For the sake of argument assume the largest AR zero, $\lambda_r = 1 - \epsilon$, where $\epsilon > 0$, is distinct. Then for moderate k

$$\rho_k \to A_r \lambda_r^k \simeq A_r(1 - k\,\epsilon) \qquad (11.4)$$

when ϵ is small. So the a.c.f. for moderate k will follow a gentle linear decline for an *unstable* series, as opposed to a rapid geometric decline for a *stable* series. Equations 11.2 and 11.4 easily generalise when there are coincident λ's.

This theoretical behaviour should be mimicked by the estimated a.c.f. and it is to be expected that a tendency for $\{r_k\}$ not to die out quickly is an indication of instability, which should also be apparent from the series plot. The unstable behaviour should again be indicated in the estimated p.a.c.f. which often has $\hat{\phi}_{11}$ ($= r_1$) close to unity.

Figure 11.3 shows what happens for the simulated ARIMA(0,2,0), or more briefly I(2) series. In (*a*) $\{r_k\}$ decreases slowly from 1, suggesting instability and the p.a.c.f. indicates an AR(1) model with

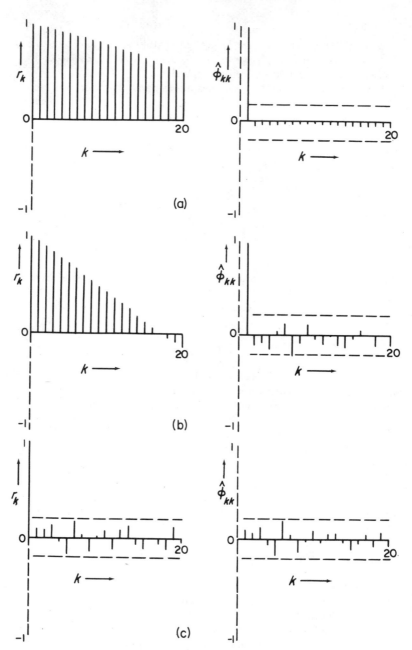

Figure 11.3   Estimated a.c.f. and p.a.c.f. for series in Figure 11.1
(a) Series; (b) 1st differences; (c) 2nd differences; (d) 3rd differences

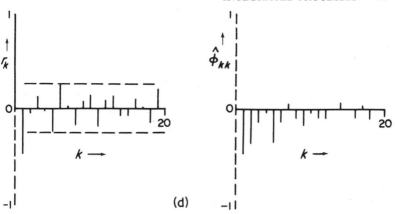

(d)

parameter ϕ approaching 1. Differencing is clearly called for. (b) shows again a linear decrease from 1, though the decline is more rapid, suggesting perhaps that the differencing has gone far enough [cf. *Figure 2.1(b)*]. However the p.a.c.f. again indicates an AR(1) with $\hat{\phi}$ near 1 (though $\hat{\phi}_{77}$ is just significant). So a second differencing is probably necessary. On doing this, an a.c.f. and p.a.c.f. compatible with white noise is obtained (c), and so the identified model would be $(1-B)^2 z_i = a_i$ (which is correct).

There is nothing to estimate in this model, and if diagnostic checks are applied, no reason emerges to modify it.

For the third differences (d), the estimated functions diverge again from the white noise pattern. In fact $\{w_i \equiv \nabla^3 z_i\}$ here follows a marginal non-invertible MA(1) model

$$w_i = a_i - a_{i-1} \tag{11.5}$$

with consequently $\rho_1 = -0.5$. *Figure 11.3(d)* shows that r_5 and r_6 are just about significant, while $|\hat{\phi}_{66}|$ looks on the large side, but otherwise the estimated functions seem compatible with equation 11.5 [cf. *Figure 5.1(a)*].

Exercise 11.1   Investigate series D* and its first two differenced series.

Solution: *Figure 11.4(a)* indicates an AR(1) model with ϕ approaching 1, which suggests differencing. *Figure 11.4(b)* shows that the differenced series could be close to white noise (though r_7 is approaching significance and $\hat{\phi}_{77}, \hat{\phi}_{14,14}$ are significant). Second differencing increases the variance from 13·06 to 30·44 and the estimated functions *Figure 11.4(c)* have moved away from the white noise patterns.

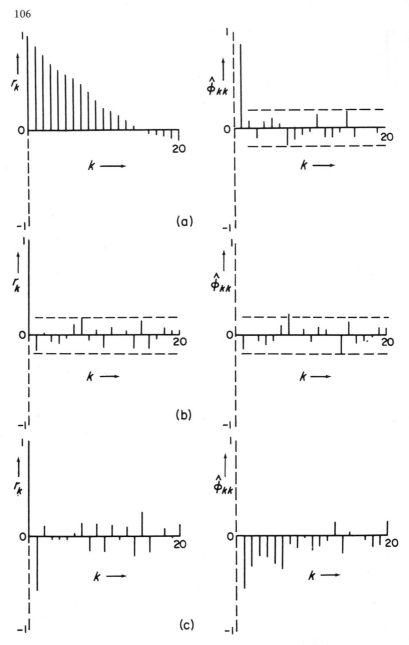

Figure 11.4   Estimated a.c.f. and p.a.c.f. for D and its differenced series
(a) Series; (b) 1st differences; (c) 2nd differences*

Exercise 11.2 Identify a possible model for series L.

Solution: The series and its first two differenced series, together with their estimated functions are given in *Figure 11.5*.

(*a*) Shows clearly that first differencing is necessary.
(*b*) Indicates a slightly wandering level.
(*c*) Though apparently stationary, has 'worse' estimated functions than (*b*).

It is concluded that the ∇z_i series should be identified. The first choice is AR(1) with $\hat{\phi}_0 = 0.422$, though $\hat{\phi}_{13,13}$ is very nearly significant. An ARMA(1,1) overfit in the region of *Figure 6.1(f)* should also be considered. For this

$$\hat{\phi}_0 = \frac{0.272}{0.422} = 0.645$$

$$b = (1 - 0.544 + 0.6446^2)/(0.422 - 0.6446) = -3.916$$

and

$$\hat{\theta}_0 = [-3.916 + \sqrt{(15.34 - 4)}]/2 = -0.274$$

$(1-0.422B)(1-0.223B) = 1-0.645B + 0.094B^2$, so these initial models are not very different.

Exercise 11.3 Using the first half of series G, obtain a simulated IMA (1,1) series and investigate its estimated a.c.f. and p.a.c.f.

Solution: Series G is MA(1), so writing $z_i = \nabla x_i$, x_i is IMA(1,1). Now $x_i = (1-B)^{-1} z_i = z_i + z_{i-1} + z_{i-2} + \ldots$ so, apart from some constant, $x_1 = z_1, x_2 = z_1 + z_2, \ldots, x_{50} = z_1 + \ldots + z_{50}$. $\{x_i\}$ is shown in *Figure 11.6*, and as expected has a wandering level.

The estimated functions indicate an important point. r_1 and consequently $\hat{\phi}_{11}$ are not near unity, and indeed, for a non-stationary or unstable series, there is no reason why the linear fall off of $\{r_k\}$ should always be from a value near unity.

The example does not appear over convincing. This is because for moderate θ, rather short series are required to demonstrate the effect[21], and then of course the sampling errors are correspondingly higher. The model for x_i here is known to be

$$(1-B)x_i = (1-0.6B)a_i$$

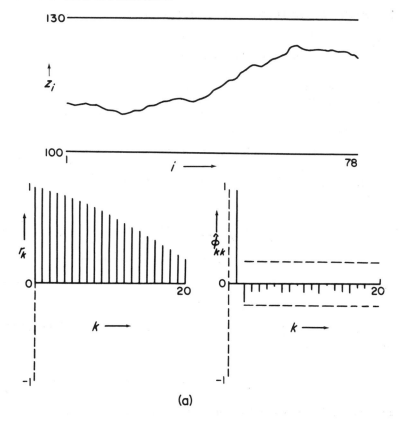

Figure 11.5   Dow Jones Utilities Index, Series L

which can be rewritten as

$$(1 - 0.4B - 0.6 \times 0.4B^2 - 0.6^2 \times 0.4B^3 - \ldots)x_i = a_i$$

and so it is to be expected that a higher order AR model could also explain $\{x_i\}$. For a less negative MA parameter, a lower order AR model should be satisfactory. So situations are possible where both of two equivalent models, AR(1) and IMA(1,1), are appropriate. Perhaps the first differenced Dow Jones series is close to this, with a chance building up of the estimated functions at larger lags [cf. *Figure 11.5(b)* and (c)].

However, if the θ value is sufficiently negative, the process can be

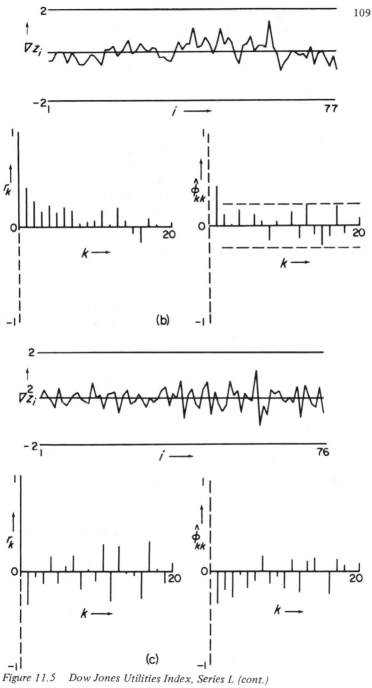

Figure 11.5   Dow Jones Utilities Index, Series L (cont.)

considered alternatively as being close to white noise. For instance, consider

$$(1 - 0.9B)z_i = (1 - 0.86B)a_i$$

which can be written

$$z_i = a_i + 0.04\,a_{i-1} + 0.04 \times 0.9\,a_{i-2} + \ldots$$

This has $\rho_1 = 0.047$, and it is evidently close to a white noise process.

Inevitably, identification methods encounter examples where the action is not clear cut. As mentioned later, the author prefers to use the behaviour of the variances of successive differenced series as a criterion for deciding on the degree of differencing necessary. This appears to have a smaller 'twilight area' where decision is difficult.

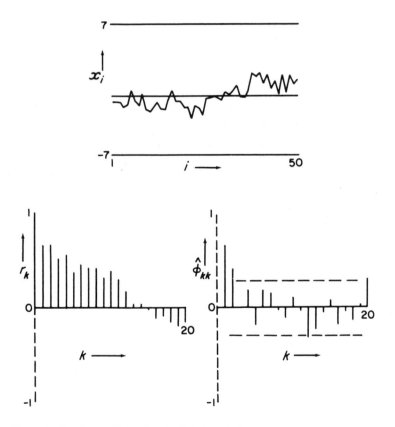

Figure 11.6   The first half of series G, integrated once

The non-stationarity of the series discussed so far in this chapter is accounted for, in the models, by zeros $B = 1$ not lying outside the unit circle.

Should a deterministic trend of degree d be present in the process, we replace w_i by

$$\widetilde{w}_i = w_i - E[w_i]$$

For if

$$z_i = f_0 + f_1 i + \ldots + f_d i^d + y_i$$

where

$$\phi(B)\nabla^d y_i = \theta(B)a_i$$

then

$$\nabla^d y_i = \phi^{-1}(B)\theta(B)a_i$$

and, after a little algebra,

$$w_i = \nabla^d z_i = f_d d! + \phi^{-1}(B)\theta(B)a_i$$

so

$$\phi(B)w_i = \phi(1)f_d d! + \theta(B)a_i$$

and taking expectations,

$$\phi(B)E[w_i] = \phi(1)f_d d!$$

so

$$\phi(B)\widetilde{w}_i = \theta(B)a_i$$

Thus differencing will remove both stochastic and deterministic trends. However, it also rapidly increases the noise variance, and so should not be overdone.

Exercise 11.4   Compare the variances of z, ∇z and $\nabla^2 z$ for the series $\{z_i = i\lambda + a_i : i = 1, \ldots, N\}$, where λ is fixed and $a_i \sim IN(0, \sigma_a^2)$.

Solution:

$$\text{Var}[z] = \frac{\lambda^2(N^2 - 1)}{12} + \sigma_a^2$$

$$\text{Var}[\nabla z] = 2\sigma_a^2$$

$$\text{Var}[\nabla_z^2] = 6\sigma_a^2$$

Exercise 11.5 Repeat for $\left\{ z_i = \sum_{j=1}^{i} J_j + a_i : i = 1, \ldots, N \right\}$, where:

1. The J_j are independent and identically distributed random variables with p.d.f. $= c(x) + \delta(x)$, where $c(x)$ is continuous with
   $$\int_{-\infty}^{\infty} c(x)\,dx = c \ll 1 \text{ and } \delta(x) \text{ is a dirac delta function}$$
   $\delta(0) = 1 - c$
   $\delta(x) = 0 \ x \neq 0.$
2. The shocks $a_i \sim IN(0, \sigma_a^2)$, and $\{a_i\}$ is independent of $\{J_i\}$.
3. There are $|J_i| \gg \sigma_a$.

Solution: The series of jumps $\{J_i\}$ gives rise to occasional random changes of level. $\mathrm{Var}[z]$ will be tedious to evaluate, however it is not really needed, since the situation is one where first-differencing is called for, and will considerably reduce the variance. Now

$$\mathrm{Var}[z_i] \quad = i\,\sigma_J^2 + \sigma_a^2$$
$$\mathrm{Var}[\nabla z_i] \quad = \sigma_J^2 + 2\sigma_a^2$$
$$\mathrm{Var}[\nabla^2 z_i] \ = 2\sigma_J^2 + 6\sigma_a^2$$

and since these last two R.H.S. are both independent of i, they give $\mathrm{Var}[\nabla z]$ and $\mathrm{Var}[\nabla^2 z]$, respectively. Overdifferencing will cause the series variance to more than double.

For this simple case there will be a sharp decrease in variance on first-differencing, but second-differencing will show up as unambiguous over-differencing. However, if condition (3) is relaxed, some increase in variance could arise from correct first-differencing. Indeed, if all $|J_i| \ll \sigma_a$, the variance could about double, and first differencing would appear to be overdifferencing. This should not trouble us too much, since for practical purposes it would most likely be overdifferencing, the jumps being small compared with the shocks.

Of course, the situation is less clear cut in practice, as one is dealing with *observed* variances, which for the shorter series can be 40% out 5% of the time (the 97·5% points of $F_{\infty,50}$ and $F_{50,\infty}$ are, respectively, 1·56 and 1·44).

Exercise 11.6 Investigate the Ben Nevis data, A* (Appendix I) and its first differenced series.

Solution: *See Figure 11.7.* Looking at the temperatures plot, there appears to be a diagonal trend which suggests differencing. (Of course the trend is only the first half of the annual cycle, so for purposes of extrapolation a differenced model will be much more sensible than a straight line regression plus noise). The differenced series looks stationary.

Again, for the temperatures $\{r_k\}$ and $\{\hat\phi_{kk}\}$ suggest differencing, whilst the plotted functions for the differenced series suggest perhaps IMA(1,2) [cf. *Figure 5.2(b)*].

The degree of differencing necessary to produce stationarity is first determined, usually by inspection of the a.c.f. For a stationary series, the ratio r_k/r_1 should die out fairly rapidly, so if this is not the case differencing is continued until it does. Then, for this differenced series, an ARMA model is fitted as before by the iterative procedure of identification, estimation and verification.

For identification, it is usual to input the original data to a modified form of the Program (Appendix II), which calculates and outputs the mean, variance, a.c.f. and p.a.c.f. for the series and its first two differenced series. The value of d is first decided, as described above, and then inspection of the $\{r_k\}$ and $\{\hat\phi_{kk}\}$ corresponding to the series $\{\nabla^d z_i\}$ (of length $N-d$), should indicate the model(s) to be entertained.

The above identification procedure appears to be very successful with a large variety of industrial and economic time series. However should the series be seasonal[†], as are many sales and meteorological series, the modifications of Chapter 12 are required. Estimation and verification go through as before, as does forecasting from the finally fitted model.

Exercise 11.7 Fit the models identified in exercises 11.2 and 11.6. Verify these fits and the *random walk* model, $(1-B)z_i = a_i$, of exercise 11.1.

Solution: Series L, Dow Jones (Appendix I).
ARI(1,1) fit:

   Estimation $\hat\phi = 0.504$ with S.E. $= 0.099$, $\hat\sigma_a^2 = 0.146$.

   Verification $\bar w = 0.065$, S.E.$[w] > \left\{ \dfrac{0.146\,(1 + 0.504)}{77\,(1 - 0.504)} \right\}^{1/2} > 0.065$.

   Residuals analysis: 2S.E. $= 0.76$, and inspection shows 4 residuals significant, which is acceptable.

   $2/\sqrt{77} = 0.23$, so $r_1(\hat a) = -0.11$ is significant by Box–Pierce and $r_{11}, r_{13}, r_{16}, r_{17}$ are also just significant.

   $\chi^2 = 29.96$ which is significant at the 10% level.

Overall conclusion: ARI(1,1) fit could be improved on.

[†]Sometimes this is not realised initially, but shows up when periodicities are observed in the residuals after fitting.

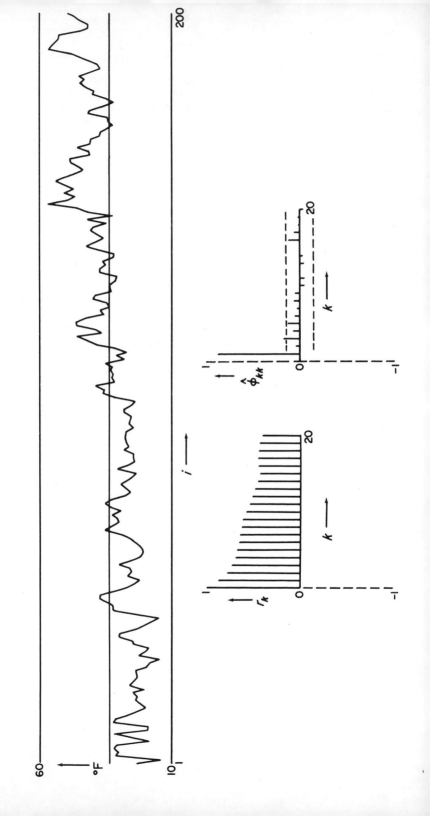

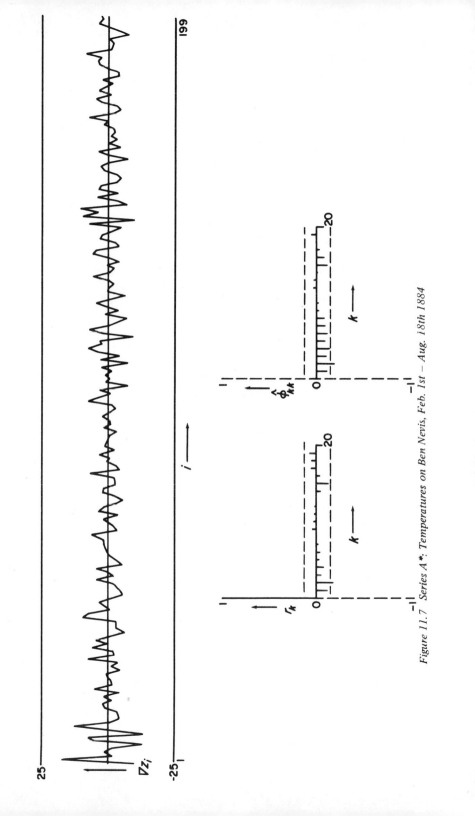

Figure 11.7 Series A*: Temperatures on Ben Nevis, Feb. 1st – Aug. 18th 1884

ARIMA(1,1,1) overfit:

Estimation $\hat{\phi} = 0.872$ S.E. $= 0.096$
$\hat{\theta} = 0.547$ S.E. $= 0.161$ $\hat{\sigma}_a^2 = 0.143$.
Verification $\bar{w}$ is not significant. Inspection shows again
just 4 residuals significant. Only $r_{16}(\hat{a})$ significant this time.
$\chi^2 = 23.47$ is not significant.
Conclusion: the overfit is an improvement and seems acceptable.

Series A*, Ben Nevis (Appendix I). IMA(1,2) fit.

Estimation $\hat{\theta}_1 = -0.238$ S.E. $= 0.068$
$\hat{\theta}_2 = -0.305$ S.E. $= 0.069$
$\hat{\sigma}_a^2 = 17.91$
Verification $\chi^2 = 17.31$
Residual analysis: There is some trouble in starting up, where
$a_1, a_2, a_6, a_9, a_{11}$ are significant and there is another bad patch in
the middle, where $a_{145}, a_{146}, a_{148}$ are significant. But apart from
these only a_{189} is significant. $r_{15}(\hat{a}) = -0.143$ which is just
significant (2 S.E. $= 0.141$), but none other of $\{r_k(\hat{a})\}$ are,
though this presents a wavelike pattern. The cumulative
periodogram is not significant. It is concluded that the fitted
model is not too unreasonable.

Series D*, I.C.I. (Appendix I) I(1) model.

$\bar{w} = -0.14$, $\hat{\sigma}_a^2 = 13.06$ so S.E.$[\bar{w}] = \sqrt{0.1232}$, and $\bar{w}$ is not significant. $\chi^2 = 19.64$ is not significant. Thus there is no reason yet
for rejecting model.
The author prefers to cut computing costs at the identification stage
by using a simple routine to determine the required degree of differencing. Then usually only one set of $\{r_k\}$ and $\{\hat{\phi}_{kk}\}$ need be calculated.
The d is found by computing $s_j^2 = s^2 \nabla^j z$ for $j = 0,1,2$ and comparing s_j^2
with s_{j-1}^2 for $j = 1,2$. For N large enough for Box—Jenkins methods to
be valid, s_j^2 decreases until stationarity is achieved, and then increases
rapidly. Sometimes $s_j^2 \simeq s_{j-1}^2$ for some $j > 0$, and then more than one d
may need consideration.
As far as a fit to the observed series is concerned, it will probably not
matter which of these d is chosen, but if the fit is required for generating
forecasts, usually the larger d will be preferable. For instance, consider
the choice between $d = 0$ and $d = 1$. If $d = 0$ is chosen, the level of the
forecasts will be for ever tied to the level of the series over the fitting
period. But if $d = 1$, updated forecasts will be able to adjust themselves to any future change in level.
There are snags with the above 'Variate Difference' method (cf. Ref.
23), but at least it must be considered as a useful extra tool. *Table 11.1*
shows how it performs with the series considered in this chapter.

Table 11.1 Variances of successive differenced series

Series	$(1-B)^2 z_i = a_i$	D*	L	G	A*
s_0^2	9360·85	75·69	30·32	1·16	85·58
s_1^2	12·34	13·06	0·18	3·45	19·60
s_2^2	1·05	30·44	0·20	11·59	44·32
s_3^2	1·93	97·21	0·54	40·96	124·22
$\therefore$ Chosen d	2	1	1	0	1
Box–Jenkins choice	2	1	1	0	1

For the ARIMA model the e.f.f. will be given by

$$\varphi(B)\hat{z}_i(l) = 0, l > q$$

with $p + d$ pivotal values $\hat{z}_i(q-p-d+1), \ldots, \hat{z}_i(q)$.

Exercise 11.8 Find the form of the e.f.f. for the IMA(2,2) process.

Solution: $(1-B)^2 \hat{z}_i(l) = 0 \Rightarrow \hat{z}_i(l) = A + Cl, l > 0$ with the two pivotal values $\hat{z}_i(1) = A + C$, $\hat{z}_i(2) = A + 2C$. Hence the e.f.f. is

$$\hat{z}_i(l) = \{2\hat{z}_i(1) - \hat{z}_i(2)\} + \{\hat{z}_i(2) - \hat{z}_i(1)\}l, l > 0$$

a straight line through $\hat{z}_i(1)$ and $\hat{z}_i(2)$, which are given by

$$\hat{z}_i(1) = 2z_i - z_{i-1} + \theta_1 a_i + \theta_2 a_{i-1}$$

and

$$\hat{z}_i(2) = 2\hat{z}_i(1) - z_i + \theta_2 a_i$$

See Figure 11.8(a).

Exercise 11.9 Find the e.f.f. for the ARIMA(1,1,0) process.

Solution: $(1-B)(1-\phi B)\hat{z}_i(l) = 0 \Rightarrow \hat{z}_i(l) = A + C\phi^l, l > -2$ with pivotal values $\hat{z}_i(-1) = z_{i-1} = A + C/\phi$ and $\hat{z}_i(0) = z_i = A + C$. Hence

$$A = \frac{z_i - \phi z_{i-1}}{1 - \phi} \text{ and } C = -\frac{\phi(z_i - z_{i-1})}{1 - \phi}$$

See Figure 11.8(b).

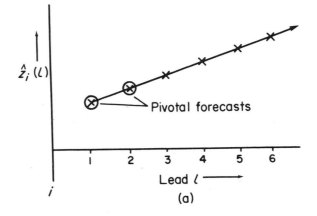

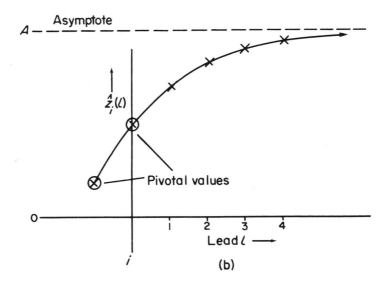

Figure 11.8   E.f.f. for (a) IMA(2,2); (b) ARIMA(1,1,0); (c) random walk fit to ICI closing stock prices

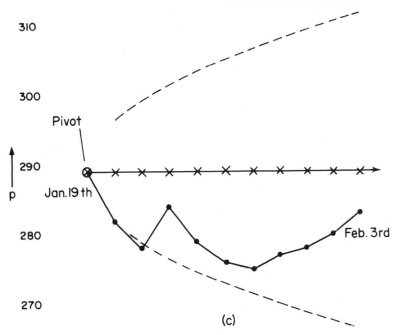

(c)

The IMA(1,1) model is

$$z_i = z_{i-1} + a_i + \theta a_{i-1} \qquad (11.6)$$

and its e.f.f. is

$$\hat{z}_i(1) = z_i + \theta a_i \qquad (11.7)$$

$$\hat{z}_i(l) = \hat{z}_i(l-1) \qquad \text{for all } l > 1$$

So the forecasts made for all leads are the same as the one step ahead forecasts, which can be written from equation 11.7 as

$$\hat{z}_i(1) = (1 + \theta)z_i - \theta (z_i - a_i)$$

$$= (1 + \theta)z_i - \theta (z_{i-1} + \theta a_{i-1}) \quad \text{using equation 11.6}$$

$$= (1 + \theta)z_i - \theta \hat{z}_{i-1}(1) \qquad \text{using equation 11.7 (11.8)}$$

This is the famous *exponential smoothing*[24] recursive formula for updating one step ahead forecasts, and the successive $\hat{z}_i(1)$ are thus obtained by interpolating between the previous forecast and the current value.

Also by successive elimination of $\hat{z}_{i-j}(1), j = 1, 2, \ldots$ from the R.H.S. of equation 11.8, we get

$$\hat{z}_i(1) = (1 + \theta) \sum_{j=0}^{\infty} (-\theta)^j z_{i-j}$$

Since $|\theta| < 1$ for invertibility, this is a geometrically or *exponentially* weighted average of previous values. Consequently the IMA(1,1) process is also called the *exponentially weighted moving average process,* abbreviated to EWMA.

We can consider the forecasts as defining a *level* for the process. Rewriting equation 11.7 as

$$
\begin{aligned}
\hat{z}_i(1) &= z_i - a_i + (1 + \theta)a_i \\
&= z_{i-1} + \theta a_{i-1} + (1 + \theta)a_i && \text{using equation 11.6} \\
&= \hat{z}_{i-1}(1) + (1 + \theta)a_i && \text{using equation 11.7}
\end{aligned}
$$

we see that $(1 + \theta)$ times the current shock is absorbed into this level. For large negative θ this will only be a small portion, but for positive θ it will be more than the shock.

For other ARIMA($p,1,q$) models the forecast level is also continuously updated, and for ARIMA($p,2,q$) models the forecast slope updates as well. For forecasting, if in doubt, it is consequently preferable to use an ARIMA rather than an ARMA model, since then the level (or level and slope) is not tied to its past value. Of course for such nonstationary models the forecast variance, $V(l)$, will diverge with l.

Exercise 11.10   Find $V(l)$ for AR(1), ARMA(1,1) and IMA(1,1).

Solution: For AR(1),

$$\psi(B) = (1 - \phi B)^{-1} = 1 + \phi B + \phi^2 B^2 + \ldots$$

So, from equation 10.5

$$V(l) = \left(\frac{1 - \phi^{2l}}{1 - \phi^2} \right) \sigma_a^2 \to \frac{\sigma_a^2}{1 - \phi^2}$$

For ARMA(1,1),

$$\psi(B) = 1 + (\phi + \theta)B + \phi(\phi + \theta)B^2 + \phi^2(\phi + \theta)B^3 + \ldots$$

So

$$V(l) = \left[1 + (\phi + \theta)^2 \left(\frac{1 - \phi^{2l-2}}{1 - \phi^2} \right) \right] \sigma_a^2 \to \left(\frac{1 + 2\phi\theta + \theta^2}{1 - \phi^2} \right) \sigma_a^2$$

For IMA(1,1),

$$\psi(B) = 1 + (1 + \theta)B + (1 + \theta)B^2 + \ldots$$

So

$$V(l) = \left[1 + (l - 1)(1 + \theta)^2 \right] \sigma_a^2$$

Exercise 11.11 What can be said about forecasts made for future I.C.I. Closing Stock Prices on Jan. 19th 1973 (*see* series D* Appendix I)?

Solution: The Box–Jenkins model is $(1-B)z_i = a_i$

so

$$\hat{z}_i(l) = \hat{z}_i(l-1) \quad l > 1$$

and

$$\hat{z}_i(1) = z_i$$

Also

$$V(l) = l\sigma_a^2 \rightarrow \infty$$

So, assuming the *random walk* model is correct and remains unchanged,

$$2 \text{ S.E. } [\hat{z}_i(l)] = 2\sqrt{(13\cdot06l)}$$

and the forecast for all future prices is the price on Jan. 19th, 289p. *See Figure 11.8(c)*, which includes the confidence lines and the actual future realisation for leads up to 10.

The 2 S.E. limit lines give rough 95% confidence intervals for the *individual* forecasts, and not for the forecast function for all lead times. As has already been seen, forecast errors are correlated and so, *locally*, forecasts tend to be roughly equally good or bad.

Note that stock prices often approximate to random walks[25], and then the best forecasts for all leads are very nearly the current values. However, with increasing lead, even if the model remains unchanged, the forecasts become increasingly uncertain.

Exercise 11.12 Fit an appropriate undifferenced model to the first 70 terms of series F* (Appendix I). Use this to produce forecasts for (a) $z_{71}, \ldots, z_{80}$, and then, assuming the next 20 terms have become available, for (b) $z_{91}, \ldots, z_{100}$. Compare the results with those obtained on fitting a differenced model.

Solution: For $d = 0$, the initial model is $z_i = 0.88\, z_{i-1} + a_i$, though $\hat{\phi}_{77}$ is significant.   The efficiently fitted model is $z_i = 0.917\, z_{i-1} + a_i$ with $\hat{\sigma}_a^2 = 1.152$. For this model, none of $r_k(\hat{a})$ are significant, even using Box–Pierce, and $\chi^2 = 14.78$. It is concluded that the model is acceptable.

The forecasts are consequently given by $\hat{z}_i(l) = 0.917^l\, z_i$ where $z_{70} = -2.77$ and $z_{90} = -0.69$. *See Figure 11.9.*

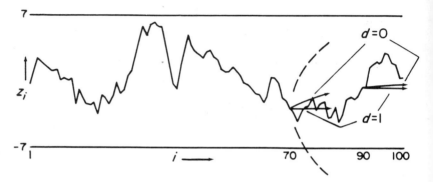

Figure 11.9   Series F* with forecasts made at i = 70 and 90, from zero and first differenced fits to its first 70 terms

For $d = 1$, the estimated functions are compatible with white noise, so model $\nabla z_i = a_i$ with $\hat{\sigma}_a^2 = 1.20$, and the forecasts are given by $\hat{z}_i(l) = z_i$. The 95% confidence lines are dotted in for (a). Since

$$1 + \hat{\phi}^2 + \ldots + \hat{\phi}^{2l-2} < l$$

$$V(l)_{AR(1)} < V(l)_{I(1)}$$

so the confidence lines for the zero differenced forecasts will be tighter. Since $\hat{\phi}$ is close to 1, the forecast functions for short leads are not so very different. But owing to the pull of the mean, for longer leads the forecasts from the stationary model, though trivial (tending to the mean), will usually do better. However, if the series instability was instead due to it being non-stationary, the differenced forecasts would be considerably superior.

The following will help in determining the forms of forecast functions for various ARIMA(p,d,q) models. Consider two functions, one of the same form as the a.c.f. of the corresponding AR(p) model, the other a polynomial of degree d. The sum of these gives the form of the required e.f.f., which is then fitted to the series in a way depending on the MA operator. The forecasts will settle down to their eventual pattern after lead $q-p-d$, (that is immediately if $q \leqslant p + d$).

It is not difficult to see why the Box—Jenkins approach, though more expensive in time, skill and computing, has proved superior to exponential smoothing. Without extending our ideas to the seasonal models of the next chapter, we have for our restricted ARIMA class (with $p + q, d \leqslant 2$) an effective choice of 15 models of which EWMA is just one. The situation is rather like one where we wish to state the numbers of grandchildren particular couples have. If we only can choose from the even integers $2, 4, \ldots, 30$ we could not expect always to be right, though very often we would be close. But if we had to restrict ourselves always to the number 8 say, we would generally be a long way out, though sometimes we would do as well. However, it is likely that in the first case we will have more difficulty in arriving at our estimate. We would need knowledge of the couples and their families, and to tot up our information systematically. For the second method one could train a chimpanzee.

12

Seasonal Models

We now extend our ideas to include the analysis of series with seasonal components. Consider the International Airline data M (*Figure 12.1*), which shows a marked seasonal pattern as well as a steady upward trend. Such a series exhibits periodic behaviour with period T. Here $T = 12$, the basic time interval being 1 month.

We introduce the (stationary) *seasonal autoregressive operator of order P*, the $AR(P)_T$ operator,

$$\Phi_P(B^T) \equiv 1 - \Phi_1 B^T - \ldots - \Phi_P B^{TP}$$

and similarly the (invertible) $MA(Q)_T$ operator

$$\Theta_Q(B^T) \equiv 1 + \Theta_1 B^T + \ldots + \Theta_Q B^{TQ}$$

and the *seasonal difference operator*

$$\nabla_T \equiv 1 - B^T$$

which when applied D times will be written

$$\nabla_T^D \equiv (1 - B^T)^D$$

A model of form

$$\Phi_P(B^T) \nabla_T^D \tilde{z}_i = \Theta_Q(B^T) a_i \tag{12.1}$$

will be called a $SARIMA_T$ model.

Then denoting the ordinary, stationary $AR(p)$ and invertible $MA(q)$ operators by $\phi_p(B)$ and $\theta_q(B)$, respectively, the general Box–Jenkins model, which allows for seasonality, is

$$\phi_p(B) \Phi_P(B^T) \nabla^d \nabla_T^D \tilde{z}_i = \theta_q(B) \Theta_Q(B^T) a_i \tag{12.2}$$

and is referred to as the *multiplicative* $(p,d,q) \times (P,D,Q)_T$ *model*.

Such a model is useful in explaining many series with a marked periodicity. Consider the airline data as it is written in Appendix I (series M) with $T = 12$ columns, each corresponding to a particular month. There is evidently correlation between adjacent values in columns as well as along rows. Both the monthly and the annual intervals are important.

If we had a long enough record, $SARIMA_{12}$ models for each column could be fitted and these might well turn out to be not significantly different. So for series M, if we think this could be so, a common columns model could be postulated,

$$\Phi_P(B^{12}) \nabla_{12}^D \tilde{z}_i = \Theta_Q(B^{12}) b_i \qquad (12.3)$$

where the $\{b_i\}$ is likely to be autocorrelated, since we expect a relation within rows, and a model of form

$$\phi_p(B) \nabla^d b_i = \theta_q(B) a_i \qquad (12.4)$$

might be obtained, where $\{a_i\}$ is a white noise process. Combining equations 12.3 and 12.4 gives equation 12.2, and of course the idea can be extended to multiseasonal series with several periodicities. Also note generalisations of the type $(1 - 2B \cos \alpha + B^2) = (1 - e^{i\alpha}B)(1 - e^{-i\alpha}B)$ for the operator $(1-B)^2$. With $\alpha = \pi/6$, this could account for a sine wave of period 12.

Exercise 12.1 Demonstrate this last point.

Solution:
$$\left(1 - 2B \cos \frac{\pi}{6} + B^2\right) \sin \frac{2\pi i}{12}$$

$$= \sin \frac{\pi i}{6} + \sin \frac{\pi(i-2)}{6} - 2 \cos \frac{\pi}{6} \sin \frac{\pi(i-1)}{6} = 0$$

The cycle of identification, estimation, verification is unaltered in principle, and having obtained an adequate fit, forecasts are made and updated as previously. However, here we have first, observing the seasonal period, to decide upon D as well as on d. It is possible to compute all the a.c.f's and p.a.c.f's corresponding to $\{\nabla^d \nabla_T^D z_i\}$ for $d, D = 0,1,2$. Again, the author prefers to compute $s_{j,J}^2 = s_{\nabla^j \nabla_T^J z_i}^2$ for $j, J = 0,1,2$ and to decide on d and D by comparing these.

Box and Jenkins decided to take natural logarithms of the Airline data, and identified a model with $d = 1 = D$, which agrees with the *variate difference* choice from *Table 12.1*.

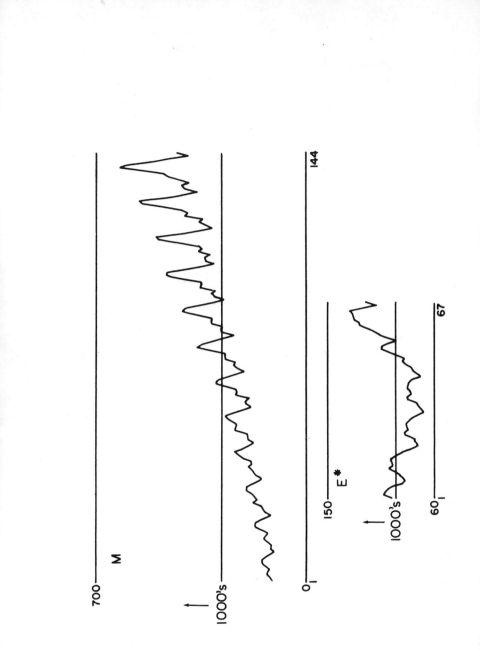

M

700

1000's

150

E*

0

144

67

60

1000's

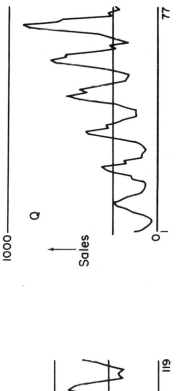

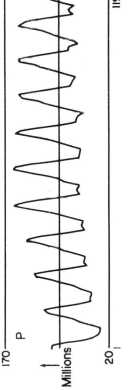

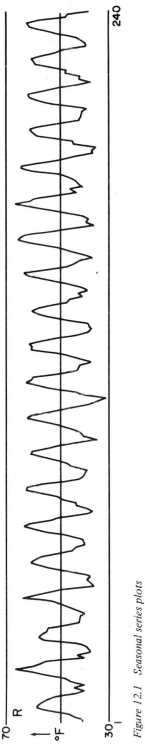

Figure 12.1 Seasonal series plots

Exercise 12.2 Write a program to decide on d and D and use it to determine them for series E*, P, ln Q and R

Solution: See Table 12.1.

Table 12.1 Variate difference matrices for series

	$D_{12} = 0$	1	2				
lnM $d = 0$	0·1949	0·0038	0·0100	E*	254	244	108
1	0·0114	(0·0021)	0·0060		23	(8)	17
2	0·0182	0·0057	0·0158		32	11	19

P				lnQ				R			
	1076	44	78		0·520	(0·054)	0·142		73	(12)	39
	332	(34)	91		0·107	(0·061)	0·163		27	19	65
	250	87	226		0·139	0·188	0·520		30	55	190

The corresponding estimated functions are given in *Figure 12.2*.

The SARIMA$_T$ model will have its theoretical a.c.f. and p.a.c.f. identical to those of the corresponding ARIMA model, obtained by replacing T by 1, except that the values will occur at intervals of T instead of consecutively. However note that for the SARIMA$_T$ model, the *unit* interval between observations is not the same as the structural interval T, but of course every observation will help to fit the model.

Because of this function sprawl, longer estimated functions are required, subject to not going beyond about $N/4$. The functions for the multiplicative model will reflect the characteristics of both the ARIMA and SARIMA components, but these will also interact giving extra terms.

Exercise 12.3 Obtain the theoretical a.c.f. for the model

$$z_i = (1 + \theta B)(1 + \Theta B^{12})a_i \tag{12.5}$$

What is the invertibility region?

Solution:

$$\rho_1 = \frac{\theta}{1 + \theta^2} \qquad \text{as for ARIMA part}$$

$$\rho_{12} = \frac{\Theta}{1 + \Theta^2} \qquad \text{as for SARIMA part}$$

$$\rho_{11} = \frac{\theta\,\Theta}{(1 + \theta^2)(1 + \Theta^2)} = \rho_{13} \qquad \text{caused by } \textit{interaction} \; (= \rho_1\,\rho_{12})$$

otherwise, for $k > 1$,

$$\rho_k = 0$$

with S.E's for the higher lag estimates given by Bartlett's formula.

The process is invertible if $-1 < \theta, \Theta < 1$ when the zeros of the multiplicative MA all lie outside the unit circle.

An easy way of obtaining the a.c.f's for multiplicative processes is to make use of the *autocovariance generating function*, A.G.F., defined by

$$\Gamma(x) = \sum_{-\infty}^{\infty} \gamma_k x^k$$

where $\{\gamma_k\}$ is the appropriate autocovariance function. Then, if the A.G.F's for any two processes are denoted by Γ_1 and Γ_2, that for their product process is $\Gamma_1 \Gamma_2$. This follows immediately from the fact (proved in Anderson[1]) that for any linear model $z_i = \psi(B) a_i$, $\Gamma(x) = \sigma_a^2 \psi(x)\psi(x^{-1})$. Exercise 12.3 can thus be checked.

Obviously multiplicative models will be more difficult to identify, and beginners will frequently need to go round the Box–Jenkins cycle more than once.

From the results of exercise 11.1, one might now be led to suspect series D* of having a seasonal component of period 7. This is rather unexpected as the stock exchange has a five day week, but it is suggested by the significant p.a.c.f. values at lags 7 and 14. Moreover, longer estimated functions show that r_{21} is significant, and $\hat{\phi}_{21,21}$ is nearly so.

If seasonal differencing appears to be necessary, the original series needs to be correspondingly longer for successful application of Box–Jenkins, the effective length being $n = N - d - DT$. Also longer estimated functions for the residuals are required in diagnostic checking. Note that the cumulative periodogram *is* an effective tool for detecting periodicities buried in a background of white noise. Useful case studies have been given[28,29,30,55,56,57].

Exercise 12.4 Obtain adequate models for series D*, E*, M, P, Q and R. (The author's fits are given at the end of this chapter (*Table 12.2*); M and Q are fully discussed by Box and Jenkins[2] and Chatfield and Prothero[27], respectively).

Sometimes more general models are required. For instance in equation 12.5 replacing $\theta \Theta$ by the less restrictive θ^* yields

$$z_i = a_i + \theta a_{i-1} + \Theta a_{i-12} + \theta^* a_{i-13} \qquad (12.6)$$

though if estimation shows that $\theta \Theta - \theta^*$ is not significant, the modification is unnecessary.

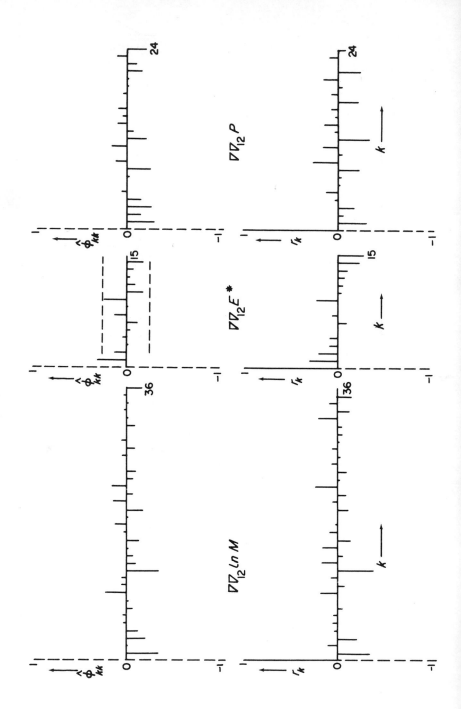

131

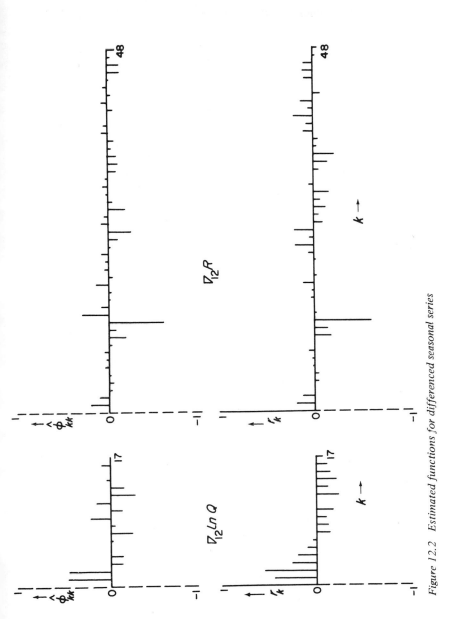

Figure 12.2 Estimated functions for differenced seasonal series

Exercise 12.5 Obtain the theoretical autocovariances for model 12.6, given $\sigma_a^2 = 1$.

Solution:
$$\gamma_0 = 1 + \theta^2 + \Theta^2 + \theta^{*2}$$
$$\gamma_1 = \theta + \Theta\,\theta^*$$
$$\gamma_{12-1} = \theta\,\Theta$$
$$\gamma_{12} = \theta\,\theta^* + \Theta$$
$$\gamma_{12+1} = \theta^*$$

otherwise, for $k > 1$,
$$\gamma_k = 0$$

This reduces to the solution of exercise 12.3 when $\theta^* = \theta\,\Theta$.

When such a non-multiplicative model is required, it is best obtained by suitable modification of the closest fitting multiplicative model, which will have been shown inadequate at the verification stage.

Table 12.2 Series fits

Series	Fitted model
D*	$(1 + 0{\cdot}186B)\,\nabla Z_i = (1 + 0{\cdot}253B^7)A_i$
E*	$(1 - 0{\cdot}349B)\,\nabla\,\nabla_{12}\,Z_i = A_i$
M	$\nabla\,\nabla_{12}\,\ln Z_i = (1 - 0{\cdot}362B)\,(1 - 0{\cdot}624B^{12})A_i$
P	$\nabla\,\nabla_{12}\,Z_i = (1 - 0{\cdot}372B - 0{\cdot}230B^2 - 0{\cdot}211B^2)$ $(1 - 0{\cdot}499B^{12} - 0{\cdot}312B^{24})A_i$
Q	$\nabla_{12}\,\ln Z_i = (1 + 0{\cdot}467 + 0{\cdot}715B^2)A_i$
R	$(1 + 0{\cdot}580B^{12})\,\nabla_{12}\,Z_i = A_i$
L	$(1 - 0{\cdot}775B)\,\nabla Z_i = (1 - 0{\cdot}373B)A_i$
A*	$\nabla Z_i = (1 - 0{\cdot}182B - 0{\cdot}238B^2)A_i$
K	$(1 - 1{\cdot}468B + 0{\cdot}591B^2)Z_i = 6{\cdot}151 + (1 + 0{\cdot}236B^{11})A_i$

Exercise 12.6 Further investigate, where necessary, the Dow Jones (L) Ben Nevis (A*) and Wölfer (K) series (Appendix I). (*See Table 12.2* for the author's solutions).

The 'efficient' fits of earlier chapters were made from a modification of a program developed by Dr D. J. Reid and Dr P. Newbold. The fits of *Table 12.2* were made using the I.C.L. package[15]. We note that there is some disparity in the results. For instance compare the fit to A* of the table with that given in exercise 11.7.

Thus, even if two independent analysts manage to agree on the model to fit, their 'efficient' programs might provide them with substantially (even if not significantly) different fits.

The reader should not then be surprised if he finds some disagreement when he identifies and estimates the series of exercises 12.4 and 12.6. Should he obtain any significantly superior fits, the author will be interested to see them.

13

Forecasting: Further Points

In many disciplines, models based on theoretical considerations are favoured to purely statistical fits. The fact that the Box—Jenkins method does not require prior knowledge of how a series is generated, but allows the observations to 'speak for themselves', is seen as a serious weakness by an economist, say. But there is evidence that Box—Jenkins forecasts often have smaller mean-square error than those based on fitting current econometric models[31,32,33], and the same is likely to be true in other fields which are as incompletely understood. An added pay-off is that usually less effort is required to obtain Box—Jenkins forecasts, as they do not require data on other variables.

However, two (or more) *unbiased* forecasts, based on such distinct philosophies, can generally be combined to form a more efficient forecast. This is because neither of the original models will be exact, but will contain different aspects of the 'truth'. The composite forecast will thus be based on more information than either, and it would be a poor strategy to adopt the best and discard the rest. A simple analogy is that, given

$$\begin{bmatrix} X_1 \\ X_2 \end{bmatrix} \sim N \left(\begin{bmatrix} \mu \\ \mu \end{bmatrix}, \sigma^2 \begin{bmatrix} 1 & \rho \\ \rho & 1 \end{bmatrix} \right)$$

$\dfrac{X_1 + X_2}{2}$ is never a worse estimator of μ than either X_1 or X_2, and, provided $\rho \neq 1$, it is better. In general the weights will not be equal, more weight being given to the forecasts with smaller mean-square errors, that is to the better forecasts, the precise values being in inverse

134

ratio to these when there are no cross-correlations between the errors (the standard statistical procedure for combining estimates). Some of the forecasts, together with their mean square errors, might well be drawn as opinions from 'experts'.

The main problem, in practice, is assigning weights to forecasts. Bates and Granger[34] suggest various ways, and recommend an adaptive method, in case the relative performances of the forecasts are changing. There is apparently no optimal way of choosing the adaptive weights[35], and Dickinson[36] concludes that owing to the large sampling errors, which occur when attempting to estimate the weights, a composite forecast will not do much better, in reality, than its best constituent. This seams to be refuted by the original evidence presented by Bates and Granger[34] and by Granger and Newbold[32]. In the latter, it was first shown that a Box–Jenkins forecast did better than one from an econometric model, to the tune of reducing the forecasting residual variance by 46%. Various combined forecasts then achieved further reductions of between 16 and 22%.

Often the investigator will have to decide for himself how a constituent forecast is likely to perform. The final $\frac{1}{3}$rd, say, of the series to date can be 'forecasted' from an analysis of the initial $\frac{2}{3}$rds, and then compared to actuality.

It would appear that Box–Jenkins forecasts are usually strong candidates for high weights. This will not be so for short series[9] or, at present, for series in which the parameters of the structural model have to be considered as changing in time.

If combining forecasts from different models leads to a better forecast, this could give a clue as to how the 'best' model might be improved. A distinction must however be made between the best fit to the available data, and the best forecasting model, estimated from this data. Often these two models will not be the same. For instance $(1 - 0.9B) z_i = a_i$ might be a better fit to a process realisation than $(1 - B) z_i = a_i$, but for forecasting the latter is likely to be preferred. Cf. exercise 11.12. Also see Chatfield and Prothero[27].

All our forecasting theory has relied on the assumption that the forecasting errors have a quadratic cost function. That is, if a forecast is off target by an amount x, the associated cost of this error will be λx^2, for some constant λ. Granger[37] shows that this is often unrealistic, the cost function, $c(x)$ say, frequently being not even symmetric.

For instance, consider a manufacturer forecasting demand for a perishable product, which sells at a constant profit p per unit, but, if not sold, involves a constant loss l per unit. In such a situation, it is unreasonable to aim at minimising the forecast variance. An underforecast, say, of $2x$ units is not 4 times as serious as one of x units. And, in general, when $l \neq p$, overforecasting will entail a different cost from underforecasting by the same amount.

Let the actual demand be y units with p.d.f. $f(y)$, and distribution function $F(y)$, and let the forecast be z units. Then the expected cost of the forecast error is given by

$$C = \int_{\infty}^{\infty} c(y-z) f(y) \, dy$$

where, evidently,

$$c(x) = \begin{matrix} px & x > 0 \\ -lx & x < 0 \end{matrix}$$

So

$$\frac{\partial C}{\partial z} = \int_{-\infty}^{\infty} \frac{\partial c(y-z)}{\partial z} f(y) \, dy$$

$$= \int_{\infty}^{z} lf(y) \, dy - \int_{z}^{\infty} pf(y) \, dy$$

$$= lF(z) - p\{1 - F(z)\}$$

Thus, for a turning value,

$$F(z) = \frac{p}{p+l} \tag{13.1}$$

and since $\dfrac{\partial^2 C}{\partial z^2} = (l + p) f(z)$, which is necessarily positive, equation 13.1

gives a minimum and so, on solving, would yield the optimum forecast z.

Granger shows that, in many circumstances, the best practical strategy is to obtain the minimum variance forecasts, as if the cost function were quadratic. When the actual cost function is non-symmetric, these forecasts are then corrected by adding a bias term, simply calculated from the cost function.

Finally, if the data have been transformed, a bias is generally introduced into the forecasts[38]. This is to be expected -- compare for instance the well-known fact that if σ is estimated by s, where s^2 is the usual unbiased estimator of σ^2, then s is a biased estimator of σ.

14

How the Models Arise

We conclude this book with a discussion of how Box—Jenkins processes can arise in practice. Many workers will only accept a fit when they can see some theoretical explanation for how the model comes about. Granger[39] has listed a number of ways in which the often encountered ARMA models could arise from AR and MA models, which are simpler to explain, and concludes that one should expect ARMA (or, more generally, multiplicative ARIMA) fits to predominate.

Should $\{z_i\}$ follow an ARMA(p,q) process, we denote this by $z_i \sim$ ARMA(p,q). Moreover, should $x_i \sim$ ARMA(p_1,q_1), $y_i \sim$ ARMA (p_2,q_2) and $\{x_i\}$, $\{y_i\}$ be independent processes, such that $z_i = x_i + y_i$, we write

$$\text{ARMA}(p,q) = \text{ARMA}(p_1,q_1) + \text{ARMA}(p_2,q_2)$$

Now, for an MA(q) process, necessarily

$$\rho_k = 0 \qquad k > q \tag{14.1}$$

That this is not a sufficient condition is seen from Anderson's inequalities, which give upper bounds to $\rho_1, \ldots, \rho_q$. Wold[40] has given a necessary and sufficient condition. A set of correlations $\{\rho_k : \rho_k = 0, k > q\}$ can arise from an MA(q) process if and only if $P(\zeta)$ has no zero of odd multiplicity in the open range $(-1,1)$, where

$$P(\cos \omega) = 1 + 2 \sum_{j=1}^{q} \rho_j \cos j \, \omega \tag{14.2}$$

It follows then that

$$P(\zeta) \geqslant 0 \text{ for all } \zeta \in (-1,1) \tag{14.3}$$

137

To show this last point, first put $\omega = 0$ in equation 14.2, then

$$P(1) = 1 + 2 \sum_{j=1}^{q} \rho_j \qquad (14.4)$$

Now the MA parameters $\theta_0 = 1, \theta_1, \ldots, \theta_q$ satisfy

$$(\theta_0 + \theta_1 + \ldots + \theta_q)^2 \gg 0$$

equality being disqualified for invertible processes, so

$$\sum_{r=0}^{q} \theta_r^2 + 2 \sum_{j=1}^{q} \left(\sum_{r=0}^{q-j} \theta_r \theta_{r+j} \right) > 0$$

or, using equation 5.6

$$1 + 2 \sum_{j=1}^{q} \rho_j > 0$$

Thus, from equation 14.4, $P(1)$ is positive, and since the Wold condition implies that the axis is not crossed in $(-1,1)$, condition 14.3 holds.

From these conditions, we can prove Granger's lemma[39]

$$MA(q_1) + MA(q_2) = MA(q) \qquad (14.5)$$

where $q \leqslant \max [q_1, q_2] = q_*$, say. (This lemma was given earlier[2].)

Proof: Provided the MA processes on the left of equation 14.5 are invertible, $P_1(\zeta)$ and $P_2(\zeta)$, and so $\sigma^2 P(\zeta) = \sigma_1^2 P_1(\zeta) + \sigma_2^2 P_2(\zeta)$, are non-negative over $(-1,1)$. Thus $P(\zeta)$ does not cross the axis in $(-1,1)$ and so does not have a zero of odd multiplicity there. It follows from Wold's condition that $MA(q_1) + MA(q_2) = MA(q)$, which is also invertible.

Using equation 14.1

for $MA(q_1)$ $\rho_k = 0$ $k > q_1$

for $MA(q_2)$ $\rho_k = 0$ $k > q_2$

Now it is simple to show that for independent $\{x_i\}$, $\{y_i\}$

$$\text{Cov}[z_i, z_{i-k}] = \text{Cov}[x_i, x_{i-k}] + \text{Cov}[y_i, y_{i-k}] \qquad (14.6)$$

so for $MA(q_1) + MA(q_2)$ $\rho_k = 0$ $k > q_*$

Thus for the sum $MA(q)$, necessarily $q \leqslant q_*$.

For any process $\{w_i\}$, denoting the corresponding γ_k by $\gamma_k(w)$, and the parameter θ_j by $\theta_j(w)$ etc., equation 14.6 becomes, for $k = q_*$,

$$\gamma_{q_*}(z) = \gamma_{q_*}(x) + \gamma_{q_*}(y) = \theta_{q_*}(x)\,\sigma_a^2(x) + \theta_{q_*}(y)\,\sigma_a^2(y)$$

so $q < q_*$ if and only if $q_1 = q_2 = q_*$ and

$$\theta_{q_*}(x)\,\sigma_a^2(x) + \theta_{q_*}(y)\,\sigma_a^2(y) = 0 \qquad (14.7)$$

This lemma enables us to prove the *main theorem*

$$\text{ARMA}(p_1, q_1) + \text{ARMA}(p_2, q_2) = \text{ARMA}(p, q)$$

where $p = p_1^* + p_2^* + h$ and $q \leqslant \max[p_2^* + q_1, p_1^* + q_2]$, h being the degree of $h(B)$, the highest common factor of the two AR operators and $\phi_{p_1}(B) = h(B)\,\phi_{p_1}^*(B)$, $\phi_{p_2}(B) = h(B)\,\phi_{p_2}^*(B)$.

Proof: Let $\qquad\qquad \phi_{p_1}(B)\,x_i = \theta_{q_1}(B)\,a_i$

and

$$\phi_{p_2}(B)\,y_i = \theta_{q_2}(B)\,b_i$$

where $\{a_i\}$ and $\{b_i\}$ are independent white noise processes. Since

$$z_i = x_i + y_i$$

$$z_i = \phi_{p_1}^{-1}(B)\,\theta_{q_1}(B)\,a_i + \phi_{p_2}^{-1}(B)\,\theta_{q_2}(B)\,b_i$$

$$= h^{-1}(B)\,[\phi_{p_1}^{-1}{}_*(B)\,\theta_{q_1}(B)\,a_i + \phi_{p_2}^{-1}{}_*(B)\,\theta_{q_2}(B)\,b_i]$$

So

$$h(B)\,\phi_{p_1}{}_*(B)\,\phi_{p_2}{}_*(B)\,z_i = \phi_{p_2}{}_*(B)\,\theta_{q_1}(B)\,a_i + \phi_{p_1}{}_*(B)\,\theta_{q_2}(B)\,b_i$$

Now, on the R.H.S., we have $\text{MA}(p_2^* + q_1) + \text{MA}(p_1^* + q_2)$, which by Granger's lemma is $\text{MA}(q \leqslant \max[p_2^* + q_1, p_1^* + q_2])$. The AR operator on the L.H.S. is of degree $h + p_1^* + p_2^*$, so $z_i \sim \text{ARMA}$ $(p_1^* + p_2^* + h, \leqslant \max[p_2^* + q_1, p_1^* + q_2])$, where the strict inequality can occur only if

$$p_2^* + q_1 = p_1^* + q_2$$

If we are dealing with *integrated* models, the main theorem becomes, for $d_1 \geqslant d_2$,

$$\text{ARIMA}(p_1, d_1, q_1) + \text{ARIMA}(p_2, d_2, q_2) = \text{ARIMA}(p, d, q)$$

where $p = p_1{}^* + p_2{}^* + h, d = d_1, q \leqslant \max [p_2{}^* + q_1, p_1{}^* + d_1 - d_2 + q_2]$ and $p_1{}^*, p_2{}^*, h$ are defined as previously.

Exercise 14.1 Prove this, assuming that Granger's lemma holds also for marginally non-invertible MA processes, whose operators contain powers of $(1-B)$ as factors.

Solution: Dropping the *argument B*, let

$$\phi_{p_1} \nabla^{d_1} x_i = \theta_{q_1} a_i \tag{14.8}$$

and

$$\phi_{p_2} \nabla^{d_2} y_i = \theta_{q_2} b_i \tag{14.9}$$

where $\{a_i\}$ and $\{b_i\}$ are independent white noise processes. Then operating on equations 14.8 and 14.9 by $\phi_{p_2}{}_*$ and $\phi_{p_1}{}_* \nabla^{d_1 - d_2}$, respectively, and adding

$$\phi_{p_1}{}^* \phi_{p_2}{}^* h \nabla^{d_1} z_i = \phi_{p_2}{}_* \theta_{q_1} a_i + \phi_{p_1}{}_* \nabla^{d_1 - d_2} \theta_{q_2} b_i$$

so

$$z_i \sim \text{ARIMA}(p_1{}^* + p_2{}^* + h, d_1, \leqslant \max [p_2{}^* + q_1, p_1{}^* + d_1 - d_2 + q_2]).$$

Seasonal models can be similarly summed.

All these results can be readily extended to cover cases where there are more than two processes on the left. For instance

$$\sum_{j=1}^{N} \text{ARMA}(p_j, q_j) = \text{ARMA}(p, q) \tag{14.10}$$

where $p = h + \sum_{j=1}^{N} p_j{}^*$ and $q \leqslant p + \max [q_j - p_j : j = 1, \ldots, N]$,

$h(B)$ being the highest common factor of all the AR operators, and $\phi_{p_j}(B) = h(B) \phi_{p_j*}(B), \ j = 1, \ldots, N$.

Exercise 14.2 Prove this.

Solution: Granger's lemma extends simply by induction to give

$$\sum_{j=1}^{N} MA(q_j) = MA(q \leqslant \max [q_j : j = 1, \ldots, N]) \quad (14.11)$$

Let

$$\phi_{p_j} x_{j_i} = \theta_{q_j} a_{j_i} \qquad j = 1, \ldots, N$$

where $\{a_{1i}\}, \ldots, \{a_{N_i}\}$ are independent white noise processes. Then multiplying the Jth of these equations by $\prod_{j \neq J} \phi_{p_{j*}}$ and adding, we get

$$h \prod_{j=1}^{N} \phi_{p_{j*}} \left(\sum_{J=1}^{N} x_{J_i} \right) = \sum_{J=1}^{N} MA \left(\sum_{j=1}^{N} p_j^* - p_J^* + p_{J_i} \right)$$

i.e.

$$\sum_j x_{j_i} \sim ARMA (h + \sum_j p_j^*, \leqslant p + \max [q_j - p_j])$$

Table 14.1 gives the various specialisations of the main theorem, where white noise is considered as ARMA(0,0) and all $p_1, p_2, q_1, q_2 > 0$. Cases where the strict inequalities apply will be rare, and are called *coincidental* by Granger[39].† We see that provided the two processes are not both MA (white noise being treated as MA(0)), the resulting sum is, in general, a proper ARMA process. Thus, for any set of independent processes, including at least one non-MA process, the sum process will almost certainly be ARMA(p,q) with $p,q > 0$. So we would expect that, in general, if we observe a process which is really a sum of non-identical sub-processes, the observed series will be fitted by an ARMA model‡, even if the sub-processes are all simple AR and MA. This is called the *aggregate* ARMA model. Again, when the observed series is the sum of the series of interest, together with an independent series of observational errors, one would expect often to obtain an ARMA fit, even when the process of interest is simple. This special case is the *observation error* ARMA model.

---

† However, for series of moderate length, *rough* coincidence, which will not be rare, will lead to the fitting of models of reduced order.
‡Of course if some of the ARMA parameters are small, it is quite likely that their estimates will not be significant and a more parsimonious *simple* fit might well result.

Table 14.1   Sum of independent ARMA processes, $1 + 2$

2 \ 1	w.n.	$MA(q_1)$	$AR(p_1)$	$ARMA(p_1,q_1)$
w.n.	w.n.	$MA(q_1)$	$ARMA(p_1,p_1)$	$ARMA(p_1, \leqslant \max [q_1,p_1])$
$MA(q_2)$		$MA(\leqslant \max [q_1,q_2])$†	$ARMA (p_1,p_1 + q_2)$	$ARMA (p_1, \leqslant \max [q_1,p_1+q_2])$
$AR(p_2)$			$ARMA (p_1*+p_2*+h, \leqslant \max [p_2*,p_1*])$	$ARMA (p_1*+p_2*+h, \leqslant \max [p_2*+q_1,p_1*])$
$ARMA(p_2,q_2)$				$ARMA (p_1*+p_2*+h, \leqslant \max [p_2*+q_1, p_1*+q_2])$‡

† Granger's lemma
‡ Main theorem

The above required independence of the component series. Relaxing this condition somewhat by writing each $x_{j_i} = u_i + v_{j_i}$, where $\{u_i\}$ is common to all components and the $\{v_{j_i}\}$ are mutually independent and independent of $\{u_i\}$, we have

$$\sum_{j=1}^{N} x_{j_i} = N u_i + \sum_{j=1}^{N} v_{j_i} \qquad (14.12)$$

where the processes on the R.H.S. are all independent, and so our theory can still be applied.

Exercise 14.3   Check *Table 14.1*.

Exercise 14.4   Show (a) $AR(1) + AR(1) = ARMA(2, \leqslant 1)$, and find

(b) $\sum_{1}^{N} AR(1)$.

Solution: For distinct, independent processes, using *Table 14.1*:

(a) $AR(1) + AR(1) = ARMA (1+1+ 0, \leqslant 1)$

(b) $\displaystyle\sum_{1}^{3} AR(1) = ARMA (2, \leqslant 1) + AR(1)$

$$= ARMA(2 + 1 + 0, \leqslant \max [1 + \leqslant 1, 2])$$

So, assuming $\displaystyle\sum_{1}^{N-1} AR(1) = ARMA(N{-}1, \leqslant N{-}2),$

$$\sum_{1}^{N} AR(1) = ARMA(N{-}1, \leqslant N{-}2) + AR(1)$$

$$= ARMA(N{-}1 + 1 + 0, \leqslant \max [1 + \leqslant N{-}2, N{-}1])$$

and so, by induction,

$$\sum_{1}^{N} AR(1) = ARMA (N, \leqslant N{-}1)$$

Or, alternatively, from equation 14.10

$$\sum_{1}^{N} ARMA(1,0) = ARMA(p, q)$$

where $p = 0 + \displaystyle\sum_{1}^{N} 1 = N$ and $q \leqslant N + (0{-}1)$.

Exercise 14.5   Specialise *Table 14.1* for when

$$p_1 + q_1, p_2 + q_2 \leqslant 2.$$

Solution: See Table 14.2.

Exercise 14.6   Simulate the following processes

$t \sim$ white noise, $u \sim MA(1)$, $v \sim MA(1)$, $w \sim MA(2)$, $x \sim MA(2)$, $y \sim AR(1)$, $z \sim ARMA(1,1)$ and identify (a) $u + t$ (b) $u + v$ (c) $u + w$ (d) $x + w$ (e) $y + t$ (f) $z + t$.

Solution: Expected identification (from *Table 14.2*).

(a) MA(1) (b) MA($\leqslant$1) (c) MA(2) (d) MA($\leqslant$2) (e) ARMA(1,1)
(f) ARMA(1, $\leqslant$ 1).

Why were the simulations in exercise 14.6 chosen so that the majority did not give rise to proper ARMA fits? Looking at *Table 14.2*, we see that, in general, on adding simple independent processes, we obtain ARMA(p,q) with $p + q > 2$, and we are concerned mainly with cases satisfying $p + q \leqslant 2$. Does this not contradict the claim[2] that generally $p + q \leqslant 2$? Not necessarily. Quite often a series of moderate length, from a higher order ARMA process, can be satisfactorily fitted by a more parsimonious model, owing to, for instance, rough cancellation of factors in the AR and MA operators, or to some of the parameters being small, so that their estimates are unsurprisingly not significant.

Also, though the observational error model is often reasonable, the independence condition for the aggregated model can be unrealistic. If sub-series have been combined, then usually it will be because they *are*

Table 14.2 Sum of independent ARMA(p,q), $p + q \leqslant 2$

	w.n.	MA(1)	MA(2)	AR(1)	AR(2)	ARMA (1,1)
w.n.	w.n.	MA(1)	MA(2)	ARMA (1, 1)	ARMA (2, 2)	ARMA (1, $\leqslant$ 1)
MA(1)		MA($\leqslant$1)	MA(2)	ARMA ·(1, 2)	ARMA (2, 3)	ARMA (1, $\leqslant$ 2)
MA(2)			MA($\leqslant$2)	ARMA (1, 3)	ARMA (2, 4)	ARMA (1, $\leqslant$ 3)
AR(1)				ARMA (2, $\leqslant$ 1)	ARMA (2, $\leqslant$ 1 or 3, $\leqslant$ 2)	ARMA (1, $\leqslant$ 1 or 2, $\leqslant$ 2)
AR(2)					ARMA (3, $\leqslant$ 1 or 4, $\leqslant$ 2)	ARMA (2, $\leqslant$ 2 or 3, $\leqslant$ 3)
ARMA (1, 1)						ARMA (1, $\leqslant$ 1 or 2, $\leqslant$ 2)

related.† But *Table 14.2* still suggests that one should be on the look out for higher order ARMA models, which can be tried as overfits.

Consequently, to explain a fitted ARMA process, the following questions may be asked:

1. Is the series really a sum of heterogeneous quantities each following simpler, distinct and independent processes?
2. Is the process simple, but contaminated by a substantial observation error series?

There is also the possibility that the process is AR, but the shocks themselves for some reason follow an MA process.

Exercise 14.7   An ARMA(2,1) fit was obtained for the number of traffic wardens off sick on any particular day in a large city, during a year in which the total numbers of male and female wardens employed hardly changed. How can this fit be explained?

Solution: The series 'off sick' can be divided into sub-series for men and women, which could be fairly independent, and could each follow a model whereby the number off sick on a particular day = a proportion of those sick on the previous day + the newly sick, which is of the form

$$z_i = \phi z_{i-1} + a_i \qquad 0 < \phi < 1$$

The addition of two such AR(1) processes would give the AR(2, 1) observed.

In the next chapter, we will investigate when it is reasonable to think a more complex observed model could have arisen from a simpler one, and in Chapter 16 we will look at a different way in which complex models can be generated.

---

†Note that for the type of dependence leading to equation 14.12, for sufficiently large N, the behaviour of $\left\{ \left(\sum_{j=1}^{N} x_{j_i} \right) \Big/ N \right\}$ is close to that of $\{u_i\}$.

15

Realisability

In the previous chapter we have seen that simple processes often give rise to mixed models. This poses the obvious question, 'How can one determine whether a particular ARMA fit could have arisen from a simple process or processes?' Or, 'Is a simple situation *realisable*[39]?'

For example, what conditions must be satisfied if

$$(1 - \phi B) z_i = (1 + \theta B) c_i \qquad (15.1)$$

is to have arisen from

$$z_i = x_i + y_i \qquad (15.2)$$

where

$$(1 - \alpha B) x_i = a_i \\ y_i = b_i \Bigg\} \qquad (15.3)$$

and $\{a_i\}$, $\{b_i\}$, $\{c_i\}$ are all white noise processes, the first two being independent?†

Operating on equation 15.2 by $(1 - \alpha B)$ and using equations 15.3

$$(1 - \alpha B) z_i = a_i + (1 - \alpha B) b_i \qquad (15.4)$$

By Granger's lemma, the R.H.S. is MA(1), so for equation 15.4 to be equivalent to 15.1, we require

$$\alpha = \phi \qquad (15.5)$$

and

$$a_i + (1 - \alpha B) b_i = (1 + \theta B) c_i$$

---

† This will be the definition of $\{a_i\}$, $\{b_i\}$ and $\{c_i\}$ throughout this chapter.

Taking variances, and then first autocovariances, gives, respectively,

$$\sigma_a^2 + (1 + \alpha^2) \, \sigma_b^2 \; = \; (1 + \theta^2) \, \sigma_c^2 \qquad (15.6)$$

and

$$-\alpha \, \sigma_b^2 \; = \; \theta \, \sigma_c^2$$

So

$$\sigma_b^2 \; = \; \frac{-\theta}{\phi} \, \sigma_c^2 \qquad (15.7)$$

and

$$\sigma_a^2 \; = \; [(1 + \theta^2) + \frac{\theta}{\phi} (1 + \phi^2)] \, \sigma_c^2 \qquad (15.8)$$

Now a variance is necessarily non-negative, so equations 15.7 and 15.8 give, respectively

$$-\frac{\theta}{\phi} \geqslant 0 \qquad (15.9)$$

and

$$(1 + \theta^2) \geqslant \frac{-\theta}{\phi} (1 + \phi^2) \qquad (15.10)$$

where the strict equalities, implying respectively $y_i \equiv 0$ and $x_i \equiv 0$, can be ignored. These can be combined to give the *realisability* condition, for a proper ARMA(1,1) to be AR(1) + white noise,

$$0 < \frac{-\theta(1 + \phi^2)}{\phi(1 + \theta^2)} < 1 \qquad (15.11)$$

Equivalently,

$$-\theta \, \phi > 0$$

and provided $1 > -\theta \, \phi$, which is certainly so for a stationary invertible process,

$$|\theta| < |\phi|$$

Exercise 15.1   Prove these alternative conditions.

Solution: Again dropping the strict inequalities, equation 15.9 gives θ and ϕ of opposite sign, so

$$-\theta \, \phi > 0$$

Equation 15.10 can be written

$$\frac{1}{\phi} (\phi + \theta) (1 + \theta\phi) > 0$$

Thus, if $1 > -\theta\phi$, then ϕ and $\phi + \theta$ have the same sign. So, when $\phi > 0$,

$$\phi > -\theta \text{ and } -\theta > 0$$

while for $\phi < 0$,

$$\phi < -\theta \text{ and } -\theta < 0$$

Thus in both possible cases $|\phi| > |\theta|$.

Exercise 15.2   Show from first principles that any IMA(1,1) process, with non-positive θ, can be considered as a random walk, $\{x_i = x_{i-1} + a_i\}$ buried in uncrosscorrelated white noise, $\{b_i\}$.

Solution: Let process be $w_i = (1-B) z_i = (1 + \theta B) c_i$. Then for $\{w_i\}$,

$$\sigma^2 = (1 + \theta^2) \sigma_c^2$$

$$\gamma_1 = \theta\sigma_c^2$$

$$\gamma_k = 0, \qquad k > 1$$

Now consider $z_i* = x_i + y_i$, where $(1-B) x_i = a_i$ and $y_i = b_i$. Then $w_i* = (1-B) z_i* = a_i + (1-B) b_i$, for which

$$\sigma^2* = \sigma_a^2 + 2\sigma_b^2$$

$$\gamma_1* = 0 - \sigma_b^2$$

$$\gamma_k* = 0, \qquad k > 1$$

Then $\{w_i*\}$ and $\{w_i\}$ are equivalent if and only if

$$\sigma_a^2 + 2\sigma_b^2 = (1 + \theta^2) \sigma_c^2 \qquad (15.6a)$$

and

$$-\sigma_b^2 = \theta\sigma_c^2 \qquad (15.7a)$$

Equation 15.7a is equivalent to 15.7 with $\phi = 1$, and using it in 15.6a gives

$$\sigma_a^2 = (1 + \theta)^2 \sigma_c^2$$

which is equivalent to 15.8. So provided that θ is negative, the required representation is always possible.

Exercise 15.3 Deduce the realisability conditions for

$$(1 - \phi_1 B - \phi_2 B^2) z_i = (1 + \theta B) c_i \qquad (15.12)$$

to have arisen from $z_i = x_i + y_i$, where

$$(1 - \alpha B) x_i = a_i, (1 - \beta B) y_i = b_i$$

Solution: $(1 - \alpha B)(1 - \beta B) z_i = (1 - \beta B) a_i + (1 - \alpha B) b_i$ must be equivalent to equation 15.12. So $(1 - \phi_1 B - \phi_2 B^2)$ factorises into $(1 - \alpha B)(1 - \beta B)$, and

$$(1 + \theta^2) \sigma_c^2 = (1 + \beta^2) \sigma_a^2 + (1 + \alpha^2) \sigma_b^2$$

$$\theta \, \sigma_c^2 = -\beta \, \sigma_a^2 - \alpha \, \sigma_b^2$$

which, on eliminating σ_b^2, yield

$$\{\alpha(1 + \beta^2) - \beta(1 + \alpha^2)\} \sigma_a^2 = \{\alpha(1 + \theta^2) + \theta(1 + \alpha^2)\} \sigma_c^2$$

So, either

$$\frac{\alpha}{1 + \alpha^2} > \frac{\beta}{1 + \beta^2} \text{ and } \frac{-\theta}{1 + \theta^2}$$

or the reverse inequality holds. Eliminating σ_a^2 similarly, gives instead

$$\frac{\beta}{1 + \beta^2} > \frac{\alpha}{1 + \alpha^2} \text{ and } \frac{-\theta}{1 + \theta^2}$$

or the reverse. So, combining

$$\frac{-\theta}{1 + \theta^2} \text{ lies between } \frac{\alpha}{1 + \alpha^2} \text{ and } \frac{\beta}{1 + \beta^2}$$

and it follows that $-\theta$ lies between α and β.

Exercise 15.4 Show that for

$$(1 - \phi_1 B - \phi_2 B^2) z_i = (1 + \theta_1 B + \theta_2 B^2) c_i \qquad (15.13)$$

to have arisen from AR(2) + white noise, it is necessary for the parameter pairs $(\phi_i, \theta_i : i = 1,2)$ to have opposite signs. Also find the full realisability conditions.

Solution: Let $z_i = x_i + y_i$, where $(1 - \alpha_1 B - \alpha_2 B^2) x_i = a_i$ and $y_i = b_i$, then

$$(1 - \alpha_1 B - \alpha_2 B^2) z_i = a_i + (1 - \alpha_1 B - \alpha_2 B^2) b_i$$

which is equivalent to equation 15.13 provided that

$$\alpha_1 = \phi_1$$

$$\alpha_2 = \phi_2$$

$$\sigma_a^2 + (1 + \alpha_1^2 + \alpha_2^2)\sigma_b^2 = (1 + \theta_1^2 + \theta_2^2)\sigma_c^2 \qquad (15.14)$$

$$-\alpha_1(1 - \alpha_2)\sigma_b^2 = \theta_1(1 + \theta_2)\sigma_c^2 \qquad (15.15)$$

$$-\alpha_2\sigma_b^2 = \theta_2\sigma_c^2 \qquad (15.16)$$

For stationary, invertible processes

$$\phi_2, -\theta_2 < 1 \qquad (15.17)$$

(*see* equation 4.9a) so equation 15.15 gives ϕ_1 and θ_1 of opposite sign, while equation 15.16 shows ϕ_2 and θ_2 are as well. Also from these two equations

$$\frac{\phi_2}{\phi_1(1 - \phi_2)} = \frac{\theta_2}{\theta_1(1 + \theta_2)} \qquad (15.18)$$

As a result of equation 15.18, which greatly restricts the possible parameter values, Granger [39] classifies the model as *coincidental*. However, this seems mistaken, since an $AR(2)$ + white noise will always yield an $ARMA(2,2)$ satisfying this condition, so there are no grounds to think the model will be rare.

Finally, eliminating σ_b^2 from equations 15.14 and 15.16

$$\sigma_a^2 = \left\{(1 + \theta_1^2 + \theta_2^2) + \frac{\theta_2}{\phi_2}(1 + \phi_1^2 + \phi_2^2)\right\}\sigma_c^2$$

so

$$0 < \frac{-\theta_2(1 + \phi_1^2 + \phi_2^2)}{\phi_2(1 + \theta_1^2 + \theta_2^2)} < 1$$

and this, together with equation 15.18, give the required conditions.

For the observation error $ARMA(1,1)$ model equation 15.6 gives

$$\sigma_c^2 = \sigma_a^2 + (1 + \phi^2)\sigma_b^2 - \theta^2\sigma_c^2$$

so, using equation 15.7,

$$\sigma_c^2 = \sigma_a^2 + (1 + \phi^2 + \theta\phi)\sigma_b^2 \qquad (15.19)$$

Now, equation 15.10 gives

$$-\frac{\phi}{\theta} > 1 + \phi(\phi + \theta)$$

and since ϕ and $\phi + \theta$ are of the same sign equation 15.19 yields

$$\sigma_c^2 = \sigma_a^2 + \lambda \, \sigma_b^2$$

where $1 < \lambda < -\dfrac{\phi}{\theta}$. This is a disquieting result since it shows that the effect of the noise variance is magnified.

Does this also happen for other aggregate models? Yes. If

$$\theta(B)c_i = \chi_1(B)a_i + \chi_2(B)b_i \qquad \text{say}$$

then

$$c_i = \frac{\chi_1(B)}{\theta(B)} \, a_i + \frac{\chi_2(B)}{\theta(B)} \, b_i$$

$$= \psi_1(B)a_i + \psi_2(B)b_i \qquad \text{say}$$

So

$$\sigma_c^2 = (1 + \sum_{j=1}^{\infty} \psi_{1_j}^2)\sigma_a^2 + (1 + \sum_{j=1}^{\infty} \psi_{2_j}^2)\sigma_b^2$$

$$> \sigma_a^2 + \sigma_b^2$$

provided at least one of $\theta(B), \chi_1(B), \chi_2(B)$ is non-trivial. If $\{y_i\}$ is noise, this can be written

$$\sigma_c^2 = \sigma_a^2 + \lambda \, \sigma_b^2 \quad \text{with} \quad \lambda > 1$$

The possibility of aggregated models introduces a new stage to the Box–Jenkins cycle — that of *interpretation.* If it is thought that an identified ARMA(p,q) model is the sum of simpler processes, then this needs to be tested. Conceptually this is a straightforward matter. We need first to estimate the aggregated model, the parameters of which will be constrained owing to the realisability conditions, and then to see whether its residual variance is not significantly greater than that of the unconstrained fit.

For the constrained model, the usual estimation procedure will need modification. Granger[39] suggests accepting the AR parameters for the unconstrained fit, and then estimating the MA parameters in terms of these. This of course is an inefficient approach, since we are overconstraining the fit by restricting the effects of the realisability constraints to the MA operator, and further research is required.

Even when the practical problems of estimating the aggregated model have been solved, there remains the problem of deciding whether the fit obtained should replace the unconstrained fit. Though, under the null hypothesis of the constrained model being true, a significance test is conceivable, it does not yet exist.

16

Autoaggregation

Two ways in which the terms of a series $\{z_i\}$ can be summed will now be discussed. Define the *autoaggregate* of $\{z_i\}$ over m time intervals by

$$s_i = z_i + z_{i-1} + \ldots + z_{i-m+1} = \left[\sum_{j=0}^{m-1} B^j\right] z_i \qquad (16.1)$$

where

$$\sum_{j=0}^{m-1} B^j \equiv \frac{1 - B^m}{1 - B} \qquad (16.2)$$

Then the *moving sum* of length m for $\{z_i\}$ is given by $\{s_i\}$, and the *period sum* by $\{s_{i_I} \equiv s_{i+(I-1)m} : i \text{ fixed}; I = 1,2,\ldots\}$, that is by non-overlapping accumulation of $\{z_i\}$ over a period of m terms.

Consider a stationary $AR(p)$ process

$$\left[\prod_{r=1}^{p} (1 - \lambda_r B)\right] z_i = a_i \qquad (16.3)$$

where, for stationarity, necessarily

$$|\lambda_r| < 1 \qquad r = 1,\ldots,p \qquad (16.4)$$

On eliminating z_i from equations 16.1 and 16.3, and using equation 16.2,

$$\left[\prod_{r=1}^{p} (1 - \lambda_r B)\right](1 - B)s_i = (1 - B^m)a_i \qquad (16.5)$$

153

Thus the *moving sum* of m terms of an AR process follows a *seasonal* model with period m, an example of the *Slutsky* effect[41].

Denoting a marginally non-invertible ARIMA(p,d,q) with degree of non-invertibility e by $(p,d;e,q)$, and similarly a SARIMA$(P,D,Q)_T$ with degree of seasonal non-invertibility E by $(P,D;E,Q)_T$, we can write the process described by equation 16.5 as

$$s_i \sim (0,0; 1,0)_m \times (p, 1; 0,0) \tag{16.6}$$

Alternatively we can write equation 16.5 as

$$\left[\prod_{r=1}^{p} (1-\lambda_r{}^m B^m)\left(\sum_{j=0}^{m-1} \lambda_r{}^j B^j \right)^{-1} \right] (1-B^m)\left(\sum_{j=0}^{m-1} B^j \right)^{-1} s_i = (1-B^m)a_i$$

or

$$\left[\prod_{r=1}^{p} (1 - \lambda_r{}^m B^m) \right] s_i = \left[\prod_{r=0}^{p} \left(\sum_{j=0}^{m-1} \lambda_r{}^j B^j \right) \right] a_i \tag{16.7}$$

where $\lambda_0 = 1$.

For the *period sum*, following Amemiya and Wu[42], equation 16.7 becomes

$$\left[\prod_{r=1}^{p} (1 - \lambda_r{}^m B^m) \right] s_{iI} = \left[\prod_{r=1}^{p} \left(\sum_{j=0}^{m-1} \lambda_r{}^j B^j \right) \right] b_{iI} \tag{16.8}$$

where

$$b_{iI} = \left[\sum_{j=0}^{m-1} B^j \right] a_{i+(I-1)m}$$

We wish to represent $\{s_{iI}\}$ in terms of some white noise process $\{c_{iI}\}$, say. As yet, this has not been done, since though the AR operator in equation 16.8 can be replaced by $\left[\prod_{r=1}^{p} (1 - \lambda_r{}^m B) \right]$ operating on I, the MA operator still operates on i. However, the R.H.S. of equation 16.8 involves only $a_{i+(I-1)m}$, $a_{i+(I-1)m-1}, \ldots,$ $a_{i+(I-1)m-(p+1)(m-1)}$, so denoting the R.H.S's of equations 16.7 and 16.8 by y_i and y_{iI}, respectively, we see that the greatest lag K, for which Cov $\lfloor y_{iI}, y_{iI-K} \rfloor$ can be non-zero, is clearly

$$q^* = \left[\frac{(p+1)(m-1)}{m} \right] \qquad (16.9)$$

where [ ] here denotes the 'integer part of'.

An important theorem[43] states that given the autocorrelations for a stationary process are all zero after some finite lag, then there is always a real MA representation for the process. Since $\{y_i\}$ is MA, it is necessarily stationary, and consequently so is its subsequence process $\{y_{iI}\}$. The theorem then gives that $\{y_{iI}\}$ has an MA representation, and equation 16.9 shows that $y_{iI} \sim MA(q^*)$ and for some white noise process $\{c_{ij}\}$, and some v_j's

$$y_{iI} = \left[1 + \sum_{j=1}^{q^*} v_j B^j \right] c_{iI} \qquad (16.10)$$

where B now operates on I. It can also be shown[42] that, owing to the inequalities 16.4, equation 16.10 is invertible. Equation 16.8 then gives, for B operating on I,

$$\left[\prod_{r-1}^{p} (1 - \lambda_r{}^m B) \right] s_{iI} = \left[1 + \sum_{j=1}^{q^*} v_j B^j \right] c_{iI} \qquad (16.11)$$

and we conclude that the period sum of m terms of an AR process follows a stationary, invertible ARMA(p,q^*).†

In fact equation 16.9 shows that $q^* \leqslant p$, the equality occurring if and only if $m > p$. So for $z_i \sim AR(p)$,

$$s_{iI} \sim ARMA(p,p) \quad \text{for } m > p \qquad (16.12)$$

For moderately large m, because of inequality 16.4 the AR operator in equation 16.11 will be $\simeq 1$, which suggests that equation 16.12 becomes $s_{iI} \dot{\sim} MA(p)$. However for large m, one would intuitively expect $s_{iI} \dot{\sim}$ white noise, and this is confirmed by Tiao[44].

The author[45] has generalised equations 16.7 and 16.11. For z_i following a stationary invertible ARMA(p,q) process

$$s_i \sim (0,0; 1,0)_m \times (p,1; 0,q) \text{ and } s_{iI} \sim ARMA\left(p, \left[\frac{q + (p+1)(m-1)}{m} \right] \right),$$

†Another example of an ARMA process arising from a simpler model.

while for z_i following an invertible $(P, D, Q)_T \times (p,d,q)$ process

$$s_i \sim (P,D; 0,Q)_T \times (0,0; 1,0)_m \times (p,d + 1; 0,q)$$

and s_{iI} follows an invertible process

$$(P,D,0)_T \times \left(p,d \quad \left[\frac{q + QT + (p + d + 1 + \{P + D\}\,T)\,(m - 1)}{m}\right]\right)$$

Owing to the fact that the observation interval for a time series is often many times the (possibly unknown) fundamental interval corresponding to any causative agency, it is to be expected that for accumulated series, such as those of production, simple AR processes will give rise to ARMA models. And often ARMA models will have resulted from *aggregating* simpler ARMA processes[46].

Exercise 16.1   For a *sampled* series from an $AR(p)$ process, find the theoretical model for the subsequence series $\{z_{iI} \equiv z_{i+(I-1)m} : I = 1,2, \ldots\}$. (Such a series is termed a *skipped* series).

Solution: By the method used for the period sum process,

$$\left[\prod_{r=1}^{p} (1 - \lambda_r B)\right] z_{iI} = a_{iI}$$

so

$$\left[\prod_{r=1}^{p} (1 - \lambda_r{}^m B^m)\right] z_{iI} = \left[\prod_{r=1}^{p} \left(\sum_{j=0}^{m-1} \lambda_r{}^j B^j\right)\right] a_{iI}$$

and

$$z_{iI} \sim \text{ARMA}\left(p, \left[\frac{p(m - 1)}{m}\right]\right)$$

This can be easily generalised. For instance, if $z_i \sim \text{ARMA}(p,q)$,

$$z_{iI} \sim \text{ARMA}\left(p, \left[\frac{p(m - 1) + q}{m}\right]\right)$$

17

Postscript

To avoid the impression that anything approaching a last word has been written in this book, a selection of ideas will now be criticised.

In the opening sentence of Chapter 1, it was stated that time series could occur in dimensions other than time. Perhaps, for instance, ocean depth along a line of latitude.

However, when the dimension is not time, an apparent problem immediately presents itself. For, although in time it is reasonable to suppose a z_i depends only on the past and present, along a line one might expect z_i to be affected by its neighbours in both directions. Happily, Whittle[47] has shown that for observations in a single dimension, a unidirectional model can always be postulated with confidence. In fact, doing this obviates the more difficult problem of estimating the parameters in an equivalent bidirectional model. So in this case, one would have got away with blind acceptance of a statement.

At the end of Chapter 6, it is implied that the only useful non-stationary models are those with zeros on, but not within, the unit circle. The example cited, $z_i = 2z_{i-1} + a_i$, will indeed *break loose* and approximately follow a geometric growth $z_i \propto 2^i$; but such a model could explain, for instance, the early stages of microbe multiplying.

Again, instead of taking logarithms, to remove heteroscadicity in situations where the process variance is increasing with the level, a mildly explosive Box–Jenkins model might be fitted. An example of this is given by Thompson and Tiao[30], who investigated a model with seasonal AR operator $(1 - \Phi_{12}B^{12})$ in which $\Phi_{12} = 1 \cdot 005$. This appears to be about one, but in fact the excess $0 \cdot 005$ is very highly significant. Taking the logarithms of series Q has also been criticised[27], other transformations appearing preferable for this data. *See* also Box and Jenkins[51].

Finally, although the Box–Jenkins approach is of undoubted value, there are other ways of analysing time series and making forecasts[35,48], and in certain cases the Box–Jenkins method will be either unacceptably expensive to perform, or indeed inferior to some other approach. Thus, if large numbers of series need to be quickly and cheaply forecast, say for stock-control or production-planning purposes, a fully automatic adaptive forecasting method, based on exponential smoothing, such as those associated with Holt and Winters[24] or Harrison[49], will be preferred. While, again, for short series with a strong seasonal component, one of these methods is likely to do better than the Box–Jenkins method, especially at longer leads[9,32]. Evidently, like other statistical procedures, the Box–Jenkins approach should not be used indiscriminately.

Having warned the reader of complacency, we conclude by indicating further areas of application for the Box–Jenkins method. The approach can be used in *process control*[2]. For, if the deviation from the target can be forecast, compensatory action may be feasible. It can be used in transfer function modelling[50], which connects input and output series. The whole approach promises to give rewarding results when extended to deal with multiseries situations.

Appendix I

Collection of Time Series (read across)

Series A*: Daily drybulb temperatures (°F) at noon on Ben Nevis, Feb. 1st – Aug. 18th 1884[4]
(courtesy of the Royal Society of Edinburgh)

22·9	13·8	31·4	30·1	31·8	31·0	18·3	23·8	31·6	18·9
18·8	31·8	31·1	27·0	23·0	19·9	21·5	23·8	22·8	24·8
20·4	25·8	24·3	22·9	23·2	23·8	19·2	18·2	14·5	22·6
20·1	18·6	24·9	25·2	30·1	29·4	23·3	20·4	17·6	14·7
24·5	32·4	32·0	33·4	37·3	36·7	31·3	26·6	23·8	21·9
26·9	25·0	25·8	30·5	25·1	21·7	20·7	21·2	22·4	24·2
25·8	29·1	35·6	32·2	29·9	30·5	32·6	29·0	33·2	35·4
32·8	27·4	25·3	27·6	29·3	26·7	24·5	23·2	30·7	26·5
23·9	24·6	24·4	28·1	26·0	27·3	27·7	27·7	27·0	24·2
26·3	25·7	25·3	27·9	27·5	25·0	23·6	31·6	35·7	35·2
38·8	31·2	32·5	32·0	33·1	31·8	35·0	27·7	31·1	26·7
30·9	38·7	41·8	45·6	36·0	38·5	46·1	46·0	42·5	35·3
36·8	33·2	34·5	39·5	38·7	32·5	33·0	33·0	30·9	30·7
37·0	36·8	34·7	35·7	31·7	32·0	37·9	42·4	38·2	35·3
38·4	40·9	39·1	34·1	41·9	32·1	41·9	45·7	56·5	49·4
46·3	50·9	47·1	50·9	53·9	50·9	45·9	43·1	45·0	48·3
48·6	40·9	41·6	45·7	40·6	40·6	37·0	36·1	33·9	32·1
34·1	34·2	41·9	39·8	35·1	31·9	34·9	39·8	39·0	42·9
44·4	42·7	45·2	41·0	37·0	37·5	41·0	45·0	47·9	56·5
55·6	54·2	52·5	52·4	44·9	40·9	41·1	44·8	46·7	49·4

Series B*: Annual rainfall (in) at Nottingham Castle, 1867–1939[5]
(courtesy of the City of Nottingham Museum and Art Gallery)

29·90	25·33	27·75	17·93	26·83	35·90	20·51	18·14	31·71	29·31
28·77	28·84	27·31	35·45	27·49	34·38	30·05	20·10	26·66	31·76
15·64	19·99	25·61	17·70	25·89	21·58	20·17	20·25	20·75	22·99
23·73	19·75	22·64	28·53	20·44	21·53	32·37	19·73	20·01	23·94
25·65	22·70	26·05	26·55	19·79	31·14	22·46	24·74	26·67	27·04
21·81	23·28	28·07	26·51	18·14	28·25	25·40	26·17	23·91	20·28
28·97	24·15	21·02	30·78	27·98	25·16	19·82	20·14	26·81	23·32
24·29	20·38	25·00							

Series D*: I.C.I. closing stock prices (new pence), Aug. 25th – Jan. 19th 1972-3[6] (courtesy, of the Financial Times)

304	303	307	299	296	293	301	293	301	295
284	286	286	287	284	282	278	281	278	277
279	278	270	268	272	273	279	279	280	275
271	277	278	279	283	284	282	283	279	280
280	279	278	283	278	270	275	273	273	272
275	273	273	272	273	272	273	271	272	271
273	277	274	274	272	280	282	292	295	295
294	290	291	288	288	290	293	288	289	291
293	293	290	288	287	289	292	288	288	285
282	286	286	287	284	283	286	282	288	286
287	292	292	294	291	288	289			

Series E*: Women unemployed (1,000's) in UK on 1st of each month, Jan. 1967 – July 1972[7] (courtesy of HMSO)

96.4	104.1	102.0	100.3	96.4	87.3	85.1	87.9	89.8	96.3
99.5	95.6	97.3	97.8	94.5	90.2	85.6	77.5	73.4	76.6
76.8	85.3	85.9	82.9	84.5	84.5	82.3	78.3	74.6	68.7
71.9	74.1	74.9	82.4	83.3	80.1	80.5	83.0	82.7	81.5
78.3	71.6	75.4	78.6	79.8	84.8	87.5	86.5	92.0	98.8
104.9	104.8	99.2	91.7	100.6	106.1	110.3	117.0	123.1	122.9
127.5	128.4	129.5	131.9	120.1	109.1	118.3			

Series F*: Simulated series, $z_i = 0.9\, z_{i-1} + a_i$, $a_i \sim IN(0,1)$

−0.26	1.32	2.56	2.08	1.81	1.40	1.17	1.33	0.14	0.45
0.17	0.43	−2.42	−0.68	−1.52	−2.38	−2.48	−2.16	−3.42	−1.31
−1.66	−2.30	−1.52	0.06	−1.18	−0.84	0.82	1.22	2.65	4.55
5.99	4.84	6.04	6.23	5.75	5.74	3.71	1.78	−0.24	−0.76
1.67	3.09	4.97	3.67	3.08	2.84	2.49	3.32	3.41	2.55
2.33	1.34	1.03	1.10	1.61	1.18	0.67	−0.21	−0.37	−0.78
−1.32	−1.37	−2.21	−1.43	0.49	0.44	−0.22	−1.72	−1.96	−2.77
−3.27	−4.19	−3.03	−2.55	−2.53	−1.57	−3.01	−2.17	−1.96	−3.81
−3.70	−2.47	−4.30	−3.40	−1.75	−1.53	−1.74	−1.39	−0.51	−0.69
1.50	1.98	2.22	1.98	3.05	2.92	1.99	1.78	0.46	0.54

Series G: Simulation of $z_i = a_i - 0.6\, a_{i-1}$, $a_i \sim IN(0,1)$

−1·23	0·03	−0·10	−0·50	0·26	1·62	−1·21	−0·57	1·34	−1·75
−0·23	0·63	0·48	−0·83	−0·03	1·31	0·86	−1·28	0·00	−0·63
0·08	−1·30	1·48	−0·28	−0·79	1·86	0·07	0·09	−0·20	−0·21
0·91	−0·36	0·48	0·61	−1·38	−0·04	0·90	1·79	−0·37	0·40
−1·19	0·98	−1·51	0·90	−1·56	2·18	−1·93	1·87	−0·97	0·46
2·12	−2·11	0·70	0·69	−0·24	0·34	0·60	0·15	−0·02	0·46
−0·54	0·89	1·07	0·20	−0·97	0·83	−0·33	0·91	−1·13	2·22
0·80	−1·95	2·61	0·59	0·71	−0·84	−0·11	1·27	−0·80	−0·76
1·58	−0·38	0·10	−0·62	2·27	−0·62	0·74	−0·16	1·34	−1·83
0·31	1·13	−0·87	1·45	−1·95	−0·51	−0·41	0·49	1·54	−0·69

Series H: Simulated series

−1·40	−2·59	−1·38	−0·27	−0·75	0·63	1·09	0·88	0·95	0·98
−0·77	−0·33	−2·15	−2·50	−1·36	−0·48	−2·05	1·46	1·13	2·85
2·67	2·71	1·30	0·88	0·07	1·47	−1·04	−1·02	2·03	2·54
0·23	−0·49	0·87	−0·61	−0·20	−0·98	−0·78	−0·80	−0·86	−1·72
−0·15	1·15	2·46	0·37	−0·80	−0·49	−0·50	−0·07	−1·92	−1·00
−2·16	−0·04	−1·91	−0·43	0·32	0·48	0·13	2·26	0·73	−0·10
1·47	0·89	0·53	0·20	0·70	0·27	−0·39	0·07	−0·89	−0·37
0·75	1·24	0·62	0·54	0·23	−1·05	0·66	−0·25	0·63	−0·91
0·21	−0·24	−0·05	−0·85	−1·55	−0·40	−1·82	−0·81	−0·28	−1·06
−0·82	0·51	−0·80	−0·24	−0·51	1·21	0·81	−0·75	−1·29	−2·26

Series J: Simulated series

0·40	−0·26	1·06	−0·52	1·79	−0·09	−0·80	−0·98	−0·35	0·59
−0·31	−1·13	0·00	−0·36	0·55	0·56	1·67	−0·84	−1·14	0·63
−0·29	−1·04	−0·87	−0·26	0·02	−0·34	−0·19	−0·25	0·80	1·02
0·52	0·79	0·01	−0·38	−0·07	0·57	−0·23	0·53	0·65	0·64
0·84	0·05	−1·04	0·35	0·21	−1·26	−0·77	−0·42	−0·64	0·88
0·52	−1·16	0·89	−0·45	−0·99	−0·81	−2·51	−1·45	−1·98	1·78
1·10	−0·34	−0·48	0·21	−0·85	−1·12	−0·86	0·47	−0·97	−0·10
−1·20	2·00	−0·65	2·57	−1·55	0·71	−0·33	0·24	0·67	1·20
−0·78	0·15	0·51	0·12	−1·72	0·01	−1·48	−0·75	0·13	0·38
−1·32	0·74	−1·48	−0·06	−0·31	0·90	0·47	0·21	−0·27	−1·96

Series K: Wölfer annual sunspot numbers, 1770-1889[16] (courtesy of Professor M. Waldmeier)

101	82	66	35	31	7	20	92	154	125
85	68	38	23	10	24	83	132	131	118
90	67	60	47	41	21	16	6	4	7
14	34	45	43	48	42	28	10	8	2
0	1	5	12	14	35	46	41	30	24
16	7	4	2	8	17	36	50	62	67
71	48	28	8	13	57	122	138	103	86
63	37	24	11	15	40	62	98	124	96
66	64	54	39	21	7	4	23	55	94
96	77	59	44	47	30	16	7	37	74
139	111	102	66	45	17	11	12	3	6
32	54	60	64	64	52	25	13	7	6

Series L: Dow Jones utilities index, Aug. 28th – Dec. 18th 1972[6] (courtesy of the Financial Times)

110·94	110·43	110·56	110·75	110·84	110·56	110·46	110·05
109·60	109·31	109·25	109·02	108·54	109·02	109·44	109·38
109·89	110·56	110·56	110·72	111·23	111·58	111·90	112·19
111·96	111·68	111·36	111·42	112·00	112·70	113·15	114·36
115·06	115·86	116·40	116·44	116·88	118·51	119·28	119·79
119·28	119·66	120·14	120·97	121·13	121·96	122·26	123·79
124·11	123·37	123·02	122·86	123·02	123·05	123·05	122·83
122·67	122·73	122·86	122·67	122·09	121·23		

Series M: International airline passenger totals (1000's)[2] (courtesy of Holden–Day Inc.)

	Jan.	Feb.	Mar.	Apr.	May	June	July	Aug.	Sept.	Oct.	Nov.	Dec.
1949	112	118	132	129	121	135	148	148	136	119	104	118
1950	115	126	141	135	125	149	170	170	158	133	114	140
1951	145	150	178	163	172	178	199	199	184	162	146	166
1952	171	180	193	181	183	218	230	242	209	191	172	194
1953	196	196	236	235	229	243	264	272	237	211	180	201
1954	204	188	235	227	234	264	302	293	259	229	203	229
1955	242	233	267	269	270	315	364	347	312	274	237	278
1956	284	277	317	313	318	374	413	405	355	306	271	306
1957	315	301	356	348	355	422	465	467	404	347	305	336
1958	340	318	362	348	363	435	491	505	404	359	310	337
1959	360	342	406	396	420	472	548	559	463	407	362	405
1960	417	391	419	461	472	535	622	606	508	461	390	432

Series P: Passenger miles (millions) flown on domestic services by United Kingdom airlines, July 1962–May 1972[26] (courtesy of HMSO)

101·6	84·3	101·5	51·0	38·5	33·7	32·2	33·1	48·1	63·2
71·5	109·4	94·1	113·9	92·9	61·8	46·0	47·9	44·9	45·5
61·1	86·1	69·5	99·2	123·5	127·4	106·2	73·2	51·2	55·9
53·3	66·8	53·2	86·6	93·7	111·7	140·4	134·4	116·9	77·8
53·4	58·7	58·3	56·1	73·4	88·0	105·5	132·6	157·8	144·2
121·6	60·3	82·6	65·3	64·8	61·5	84·8	91·5	112·7	129·9
157·7	133·8	153·5	92·5	62·5	61·5	60·6	59·6	74·2	88·0
103·1	154·9	128·4	147·1	123·4	85·1	66·4	65·4	64·2	55·0
74·5	110·5	92·6	122·5	146·8	149·5	127·5	96·5	74·1	72·2
70·6	81·0	66·8	95·7	114·5	124·0	149·1	149·0	131·8	100·9
77·6	63·6	76·8	68·1	86·2	99·3	111·6	124·5	149·6	143·3
131·3	70·9	100·4	76·4	76·8	68·8	90·5	102·6	128·3	

Series Q: Sales of company X, Jan. 1965–May 1972[27] (courtesy of Dr C. Chatfield)

154	96	73	49	36	59	95	169	210	278	298	245
200	118	90	79	78	91	167	169	289	347	375	203
223	104	107	85	75	99	135	211	335	460	488	326
346	261	224	141	148	145	223	272	445	560	612	467
518	404	300	210	196	186	247	343	464	680	711	610
613	392	273	322	189	257	324	404	677	858	895	664
628	308	324	248	272							

Series R: Mean monthly air temperature (°F) at Nottingham Castle, Jan. 1920–Dec. 1939[5] (courtesy of the City of Nottingham Museum and Art Gallery)

40·6	42·9	57·0	56·8	49·2	38·3	40·0	38·1	57·5	60·4	50·9	41·0	41·6	43·0	53·8	62·1	54·2	40·4	44·2	43·9	58·1	61·4	52·4	42·4
40·8	39·8	54·2	54·3	52·7	45·5	40·5	36·3	46·7	60·5	56·4	43·9	37·1	45·5	56·2	63·5	60·8	46·9	42·6	36·4	49·6	61·8	59·0	47·8
44·4	44·2	39·7	54·3	64·2	53·2	40·8	39·2	41·6	54·7	62·2	53·1	41·2	37·1	45·5	56·2	65·5	53·4	43·5	37·3	41·6	56·3	59·6	52·4
46·7	39·8	42·8	47·1	59·6	57·7	45·1	43·4	39·8	50·3	60·5	56·9	46·9	38·4	40·6	47·3	64·9	59·6	47·1	35·0	41·3	50·9	60·4	58·0
54·1	45·1	37·5	41·8	54·4	60·8	53·8	43·4	39·4	42·3	55·4	62·5	51·2	38·4	42·4	43·6	60·1	66·5	50·0	44·0	40·8	41·4	57·0	60·7
58·5	47·0	38·7	41·7	49·2	58·2	59·4	48·9	38·5	35·2	50·2	60·3	60·4	46·5	38·4	41·8	50·2	60·4	60·5	43·9	41·0	37·1	50·7	61·8
57·7	54·1	39·5	41·8	36·6	56·4	63·5	50·6	45·3	40·8	43·0	59·8	60·1	53·5	40·3	36·2	42·1	59·2	64·6	52·7	38·4	42·1	47·8	58·2
56·4	58·7	42·1	40·1	37·6	49·8	61·0	56·8	47·1	41·1	37·3	49·2	61·6	58·4	44·6	39·3	35·6	51·2	64·0	58·6	47·4	41·2	39·2	46·7
54·3	66·3	55·7	42·9	39·3	44·4	53·0	62·5	51·7	42·8	34·8	42·9	57·0	60·6	50·9	44·5	39·4	42·8	56·8	60·0	54·1	47·3	39·4	46·6
50·5	59·9	57·8	45·8	37·5	43·6	50·0	62·0	55·0	47·3	31·3	41·9	50·9	58·2	57·0	48·7	38·2	45·8	48·6	61·1	58·6	46·6	40·9	37·8

Appendix II

Identification program

```
'BEGIN''INTEGER'N,D1,D,T,K,NL,L,LAMDA,M,N1,I,J,J1,
'REAL' WBAR,SUM,P,Q;
START: N:=READ; 'IF' N<0 'THEN''GOTO'STOP; D1:=READ; D:=READ;
      T:=READ; K:=READ; NL:=READ; L:=READ; LAMDA:=READ; M:=READ;
      WRITETEXT(('NUMBER%OF%OBSERVATIONS%%%%%%%%%%%%%%%')');
      PRINT(N,3,0); NEWLINE(1);
      WRITETEXT(('DEGREE%OF%NONSEASONAL%DIFFERENCING%%%')');
      PRINT(D1,2,0); NEWLINE(1);
      WRITETEXT(('DEGREE%OF%SEASONAL%DIFFERENCING%%%%%%')');
      PRINT(D,2,0); NEWLINE(1);
      WRITETEXT(('PERIOD%OF%SEASONALITY%%%%%%%%%%%%%%%%')');
      PRINT(T,2,0); NEWLINE(1);
      WRITETEXT(('MAXIMUM%LAG%OF%ACF%%%%%%%%%%%%%%%%%%%')');
      PRINT(K,2,0); NEWLINE(1);
      WRITETEXT(('MAXIMUM%LAG%OF%PACF%%%%%%%%%%%%%%%%%%')');
      PRINT(L,2,0);NEWLINE(1);
      WRITETEXT(('TRANSFORMATION%PARAMETERS%%LAMDA,,M%%%')');
      PRINT(LAMDA,2,0); WRITETEXT('(',')'); PRINT(M,2,0);
      NEWLINE(2);

      N1:=N–D1–T*D;
```

```
'BEGIN'"ARRAY'Z[1:N], Z1[1:N], A[0:D], A1[0:D], B[0:(D+1)*(D+1)−1],
B1[0:(D+1)*(D1+1)−1],W[1:N],C[0:K], R[0:K],TH[1:L,1:L];
'INTEGER' 'PROCEDURE' EVEN(I); 'VALUE' I; 'INTEGER' I;
'EXTERNAL';
'INTEGER' 'PROCEDURE' FACT(X);
          'VALUE' X;
          'INTEGER'X;
          'BEGIN'"INTEGER'I,J;
              J:=1;
              'FOR'I:=X'STEP'−1'UNTIL'1'DO'J:= J*I;
              FACT:=J;
          'END';
'FOR'I:=1 'STEP'1'UNTIL'N'DO'Z[I]:=READ;
WRITETEXT('('TIME%SERIES%VALUES')'); NEWLINE(1);
J1:=0;
'FOR'J:=1'STEP'1'UNTIL'N'DO'
'BEGIN'J1:=J1+1;'IF'J1=NL+1'THEN'"BEGIN'J1:=1;NEWLINE(1);
                                          'END';
          PRINT(Z[J],4,2);
'END'; NEWLINE(2);
'IF'LAMDA=0'THEN'
'BEGIN'"FOR'I:=1'STEP'1'UNTIL'N'DO'Z1[I]:=LN(Z[I]+M);
'END'ELSE'
'BEGIN'"FOR'I:=1'STEP'1'UNTIL'N'DO'Z1[I]:=(Z[I]+M)↑LAMDA;
'END';
'FOR'I:=D1+D*T+1'STEP'1'UNTIL'N'DO'
```

```
'BEGIN' 'FOR'J:=0'STEP'1'UNTIL'D'DO'
  'BEGIN' 'A[J]:=I-J*T;
    A1[J]:=(FACT(D)/(FACT(J)*FACT(D-J)))*EVEN(J);
  'END';
  'FOR'J1:=0'STEP'1'UNTIL'D'DO'
  'FOR'J:=0'STEP'1'UNTIL'D1'DO'
  'BEGIN'B[J1*(D1+1)+J]:=A[J1]-J;
    B1[J1*(D1+1)+J]:=(A1[J1]*FACT(D1)*EVEN(J))
                      /(FACT(J)*FACT(D1-J));
  'END';
  J1:=I-D1-D*T;
  W[J1]:=0;
  'FOR'J:=0'STEP'1'UNTIL'(D+1)*(D1+1)-1'DO'
  W[J1]:=W[J1]+Z1[B[J]]*B1[J];
'END';
WRITETEXT('('VALUES%OF%DIFFERENCED%AND%TRANSFORMED%SERIES%
%')'); NEWLINE(1);
J1:=0;
'FOR'J:=1'STEP'1'UNTIL'N1'DO'
'BEGIN'J1:=J1+1;'IF'J1=NL+1'THEN' 'BEGIN'J1:=1;NEWLINE(1);
                                         'END';
  PRINT(W[J],4,2);
'END';NEWLINE(2);
WRITETEXT('('NUMBER%OF%W%VALUES%6%%%%%%')');
PRINT(N1,3,0);NEWLINE(1);
WBAR:=0;
```

```
'FOR'J:=1'STEP'1'UNTIL'N1'DO'
WBAR:=WBAR+W[J] ;
WBAR:=WBAR/N1;
WRITETEXT('('MEAN%OF%W%SERIES%%%%%%%%%%')');
PRINT(WBAR,3,2);NEWLINE(1);
'FOR'J:=0'STEP'1'UNTIL'K'DO'
'BEGIN'SUM:=0;
     'FOR'J1:= 1'STEP'1'UNTIL'N1−J'DO'
          SUM:=SUM+(W[J1]−WBAR)*(W[J1+J] −WBAR);
     C[J] :=SUM/N1;
'END';
WRITETEXT('('VARIANCE%OF%W%SERIES%%%%%')');
PRINT(C[0],3,2); NEWLINE(2);
'FOR'J:=0'STEP'1'UNTIL'K'DO'R[J] :=C[J]/C[0];
WRITETEXT('('ACF%OF%W%SERIES%')');NEWLINE(1);
J1:=0;
'FOR'J:=1'STEP'1'UNTIL'K'DO'
'BEGIN'J1:=J1+1;'IF'J1=NL+1'THEN''BEGIN'J1:=1;NEWLINE(1);
                                          'END';
     PRINT(R[J],3,3);
'END';NEWLINE(2);
TH[1,1]:=R[1] ;
'FOR'J:=2'STEP'1'UNTIL'L'DO'
'BEGIN' P:=0; Q:=0;
          'FOR'J1:=1'STEP'1'UNTIL'J−1'DO'
```

```
                    'BEGIN'P:=P+TH[J−1,J1] *R[J−J1] ;
                           Q:=Q+TH[J−1,J1] *R[J1] ;

                    'END';
                    TH[J,J]:=(R[J] −P)/(1−Q);
                    'FOR'J1:=2'STEP'1'UNTIL'J−1'DO'
                           TH[J,J1]:=TH[J−1,J1] −TH[J,J] *TH[J−1,J−J1] ;

             'END';
             WRITETEXT('('PACF%OF%W%SERIES%')');NEWLINE(1);
             J1:=0;
             'FOR'J:=1'STEP'1'UNTIL'L'DO'
             'BEGIN'J1:=J1+1;'IF'J1=NL+1'THEN''BEGIN'J1:=1;NEWLINE(1);
                                                       'END';

                    PRINT(TH[J,J],3,3);

             'END';
      'END';PAPERTHROW;
      'GOTO'START;

STOP:
'END';
```

Input Format:

Data for 1st series

$\left\{\begin{array}{l}\text{length of series }N\text{, degree of unit differencing }d,\\ \text{degree of period differencing }D\text{ (zero for non-}\\ \text{seasonal series), period of seasonality }T\text{ (zero}\\ \text{say for non-seasonal series), max. lag for a.c.f.}\\ K\text{, no. of values per line in output }NL\text{, max. lag}\\ \text{for p.a.c.f. }L\ (\leqslant K)\text{, transformation parameters}\end{array}\right.$

$$\lambda, m \ (\text{where } z_i \to (z_i+m)^\lambda \quad \lambda \neq 0$$
$$\to \ln(z_i+m) \quad \lambda = 0$$

and for no transformation $(\lambda, m) = (1,0)$,

series values $z_1, \ldots, z_N$

Data for 2nd series   {ditto}

.   .   .

Data for last series   {ditto} , terminator $(-1$, say$)$.

Appendix III
Inequality proof

$$|\rho_1| \leqslant \cos\left(\frac{\pi}{q+2}\right) \text{ for any MA}(q) \text{ process.} \tag{1}$$

Proof: Consider any set of finite real MA(q) weights $\theta_0 = 1, \theta_1, \ldots,$ $\theta_{q-1}, \theta_q \neq 0$, and extend the set by $\theta_{q+1} = 0$. Then equation 5.6 gives

$$\rho_1 = \sum_{r=0}^{q} \theta_r\theta_{r+1} \Big/ \sum_{r=0}^{q} \theta_r^2 \tag{2}$$

and from the Cauchy–Schwarz inequality

$$|\rho_1| < 1 \tag{3}$$

Differentiating equation 2 with respect to θ_r for $r = 1, \ldots, q$ gives

$$\frac{\partial\rho_1}{\partial\theta_r} = \frac{\theta_{r-1} + \theta_{r+1}}{\Sigma\theta_r^2} - \frac{2\theta_r\rho_1}{\Sigma\theta_r^2} \tag{4}$$

So, since $\Sigma\,\theta_r^2 \neq 0$,

$$\frac{\partial\rho_1}{\partial\theta_r} = 0 \tag{5}$$

when ρ_1 is given by

$$\theta_{r+1} - 2\rho_1\theta_r + \theta_{r-1} = 0 \tag{6}$$

Denoting such values of ρ_1 by $\cos\alpha$, when equation 5 holds, after differentiating equation 4 with respect to θ_r, one gets

$$\frac{\partial^2\rho_1}{\partial\theta_r^2} = -\frac{2\cos\alpha}{\Sigma\,\theta_r^2} \tag{7}$$

173

So $\rho_1 = \cos \alpha$ gives a maximum when $\cos \alpha > 0$ and satisfies equation 6. Now the general solution of equation 6 is

$$\theta_r = C \cos r\alpha + D \sin r\alpha \qquad (8)$$

and the constants, obtained from the end constraints, are

$$\theta_0 = C$$

$$0 = C \cos (q + 1) \alpha + D \sin (q + 1) \alpha$$

So equation 8 becomes

$$\theta_r = \sin (q + 1 - r) \alpha / \sin (q + 1) \alpha \qquad (9)$$

Substituting into equation 2 gives

$$\cos \alpha = \sum_0^q \sin (q + 1 - r) \alpha \sin (q - r) \; \alpha \Big/ \sum_0^q \sin^2 (q + 1 - r)\alpha$$

and, replacing $\sin (q - r) \alpha$ by $\sin (q + 1 - r) \alpha \cos \alpha - \cos (q + 1 - r) \alpha \sin \alpha$, this yields

$$0 = \sin (q + 1) \alpha \sin (q + 2)\alpha \qquad (10)$$

Since $\alpha \neq k\pi/(q+1)$, for any integer k, (equality would give infinite θ_r by equation 9), it is concluded that

$$\alpha = \frac{k\pi}{q + 2}$$

for all integers k except multiples of $(q + 2)$ which are excluded by equation 3.

The maximum value of ρ_1 is thus $\cos\left(\dfrac{\pi}{q + 2}\right)$, since this is > 0 and $\geq \cos\left(\dfrac{k\pi}{q + 2}\right)$, for all k which are not multiples of $q + 2$. So (1) is proved.

References

1. Anderson, O. D., *Spectral Analysis of Time Series,* Proposed book, 1974
2. Box, G. E. P. and Jenkins, G. M., *Time Series Analysis Forecasting and Control,* Holden-Day, San Francisco (1970)
3. Granger, C. W. J., 'The Effect of Varying Month-Length on the Analysis of Economic Time Series', *L'Industria* (Milan), 41-53 (1963)
4. Buchan, A., 'Meteorology of Ben Nevis', *Trans. R. Soc. Edinb.,* **34** (1890)
5. 'Meteorology of Nottingham', *City Engineer and Surveyor,* 1920-1939
6. *Financial Times,* Aug. 26th 1972 – Jan. 20th 1973
7. 'Unemployment Flow Statistics', *Dept. of Employment Gazette, HMSO,* Sept. 1972, 793-795
8. Parzen, E., *Stochastic Processes,* Holden-Day, San Francisco (1962)
9. Reid, D. J., 'A Comparison of Forecasting Techniques on Economic Time Series', *Forecasting in Action.* Ed. M. J. Bramson *et al.* Op. Res. Society (1972)
10. Bartlett, M. S., 'On the Theoretical Specification of Sampling Properties of Autocorrelated Time Series', *J. R. statist. Soc.,* **B 8,** 27–41 (1946)
11. Anderson, R. L., 'Distribution of the Serial Correlation Coefficient, *Ann. math. Statist.,* **13,** 1-13 (1942)
12. Jenkins, G.M. and Watts, D. G., *Spectral Analysis and Its Applications,* Holden-Day, San Francisco (1968)
13. Quenouille, M. H., 'Approximate Tests of Correlation in Time Series', *J. R. statist. Soc.,* **B11,** 68-84 (1949)
14. Anderson, O. D., 'An Inequality with a Time Series Application', privately circulated paper, 1972 (To appear in *J. Econometrics,* 1974)

15.   I.C.L. 1900 Series, Technical Publication 4284. Nov. 1972
16.   Waldmeier, M., *The Sunspot Activity in the Years 1610-1960,* Schulthess, Zürich (1961)
17.   Mann, H. B. and Wald, A., 'On Stochastic Limit and Order Relationships', *Ann. math. Statist.,* **14**, 217-226 (1943)
18.   Box, G. E. P. and Pierce, D. A., 'Distribution of Residual Auto-correlations in Autoregressive-Integrated Moving Average Time Series Models', *J. Am. statist. Ass.,* **65**, 1509-1526 (1970)
19.   Siegel, S., *Nonparametric Statistics for the Behavioral Sciences,* McGraw-Hill, New York (1956)
20.   Granger, C. W. J., 'Multi-Step Forecast Errors and Model Mis-specification'. Paper presented to the Econometric Society, Oslo, Aug. 1973
21.   Wichern, D. W., 'The Behaviour of the Sample Autocorrelation Function for an Integrated Moving Average Process', *Biometrika,* **60**, 235-239 (1973)
22.   Anderson, O. D., 'A Short Cut in Box—Jenkins Identification' Submitted for publication, 1974
23.   Tintner, G., *The Variate Difference Method,* Cowles Comm. Res. Econ. (Bloomington, Indiana), Monogr. No. 5 (1940)
24.   Winters, P. R., 'Forecasting Sales by Exponentially Weighted Moving Averages', *Man. Sci.,* **6**, 324-342 (1960)
25.   Granger, C. W. J., 'Empirical Studies of Capital Markets: A Survey', *Mathematical Methods in Investment and Finance.* Ed. Szegö and Shell. North-Holland. 1972
26.   *Monthly Digest of Statistics,* HMSO, Sept. 1973
27.   Chatfield, C. and Prothero, D. L., 'Box—Jenkins Seasonal Fore-casting: Problems in a Case-study' (With discussion), *J. R. statist. Soc.,* **A136**, 295-336 (1973)
28.   Leuthold, R. M., MacCormick, A. J. A., Schmitz, A. and Watts, D. G., 'Forecasting Daily Hog Prices and Quantities: A Study of Alternative Forecasting Techniques', *J. Am. statist. Ass.,* **65**, 90-107 (1970)
29.   Trivedi, P. K., 'Retail Inventory Investment Behaviour', *J. Econometrics,* **1**, 61-80 (1973)
30.   Thompson, H. E. and Tiao, G. C., 'Analysis of Telephone Data: A Case Study of Forecasting Seasonal Time Series', *Bell J. Econ. Man. Sci.,* **2**, 515-541 (1971)
31.   Cooper, R. L., 'The Predictive Performance of Quarterly Eco-nometric Models of the United States', *Econometric Models of Cyclical Behaviour.* Ed. B. G. Hickman. Columbia University Press (1972)

32. Granger, C. W. J. and Newbold, P., 'Economic Forecasting – the Atheist's Viewpoint'. Paper presented at a Conference on the Modelling of the U.K. Economy, London Graduate School of Business Studies (1972)

33. Naylor, T. H., Seaks, T. G. and Wichern, D. W., 'Box–Jenkins Methods: An Alternative to Econometric Models', *Int. Statist. Rev.*, **40**, 123-137, (1972)

34. Bates, J. M. and Granger, C. W. J., 'The Combination of Forecasts', *Op. Res. Q.*, **20**, 451-468 (1969)

35. Granger, C. W. J., 'Statistical Forecasting of Economic Series: A Review of Techniques', *Surrey Papers in Economics*, No. 8 (1973)

36. Dickinson, J. P., 'Some Statistical Results in the Combination of Forecasts', *Op. Res. Q.*, **24**, 253-260, (1973)

37. Granger, C. W. J., 'Prediction with a Generalised Cost of Error Function', *Op. Res. Q.*, **20**, 199-207 (1969)

38. Granger, C. W. J. and Newbold, P., 'Forecasting Transformed Variables', Nottingham Forecasting Project, Note 6 (1970)

39. Granger, C. W. J., 'Time Series Modelling and Interpretation'. Paper presented at the European Econometric Congress, Budapest (Sept. 1972)

40. Wold, H., *A Study in the Analysis of Stationary Time Series*, 2nd edn, Almqvist and Wiksell, Stockholm (1954)

41. Slutsky, E., 'The Summation of Random Causes as the Source of Cyclic Processes', *Econometrika*, **5** (1937)

42. Amemiya, T. and Wu, R. Y., 'The Effect of Aggregation on Prediction in the Autoregressive Model', *J. Am. statist. Ass.*, **67**, 628-632 (1972)

43. Anderson, T. W., *Statistical Analysis of Time Series*, Wiley, New York (1971)

44. Tiao, G. C., 'Asymptotic Behaviour of Temporal Aggregates of Time Series', *Biometrika*, **59**, 525-531 (1972)

45. Anderson, O. D., 'Autoaggregation in Box–Jenkins Models'. Unpublished M.Sc. project, University of Nottingham (1972)

46. Brewer, K. R. W., 'Some Consequences of Temporal Aggregation and Systematic Sampling for ARMA and ARMAX Models, *J. Econometrics*, **1**, 133-154 (1973)

47. Whittle, P., 'On Stationary Processes in the Plane', *Biometrika*, **41**, 434-449 (1954)

48. Anderson, O. D., *Comparative Forecasting and Time Series Analysis*. Submitted for publication, 1974

49. Harrison, P. J., 'Short Term Sales Forecasting', *J. R. statist. Soc.*, **C14**, 102-139 (1965)

50. Anderson, O. D., *Statistical Transfer Function Modelling.* Submitted for publication, 1974

51. Box, G. E. P. and Jenkins, G. M., 'Some Comments on a Paper by Chatfield and Prothero and on a Review by Kendall' (With reply), *J. R. statist. Soc.,* **A136**, 337-352 (1973)

52. Newbold, P. and Granger, C. W. J., 'Experience with Forecasting Univariate Time Series and the Combination of Forecasts'. To be read before R. statist. Soc., Jan. 1974

53. Neave, H., 'Random Number Package', *Computer Applications in the Natural and Social Sciences,* Nottingham University (1972)

54. Box, G. E. P., and Cox, D. R., 'An Analysis of Transformations' (With discussion), *J. R. statist. Soc.,* **B26**, 211-252 (1964)

55. Makridakis, S. and Wheelwright, S., The Box–Jenkins Method of Forecasting', *Eur. Mktng Rev.,* **7**, 1-18 (1972)

56. Tomasek, O., 'Statistical Forecasting of Telephone Time Series', *ITO Telecommunication J.* (Geneva), 1-7 (Dec. 1972)

57. Mabert, V. A. and Radcliffe, R. C., 'A Forecasting Methodology as Applied to Financial Time Series', *Accounting Rev.,* 61-75 (Jan. 1974)

Index

A.c.f., *see* Autocorrelation function
A.G.F., 129
Accumulated series, 1, 156
Admissibility, 56–8
Aggregate ARMA model, 141
Amemiya, T., 154
Anderson, O. D., 58, 129, 137, 155, 175–8
Anderson, R. L., 78, 175
Anderson, T. W., 177
Autoaggregation, 153–6
Autocorrelation, 4, 6–11
  estimate of, 6
  standard error of, 8
Autocorrelation function, 4
  constraints on, 9
  for AR(1), 4, 16–8
  for AR(2), 20–3, 26
  for AR(p), 26, 29–30
  for ARMA(1, 1), 45–51
  for ARMA (p, q), 44–5
  for ARIMA (p, d, q), 103
  for MA(1), 32, 34–5
  for MA(2), 37–41
  for MA(q), 42
  for unstable process, 103
  for white noise, 13
  sampling properties, 6–7
Autocorrelation matrix, 9
Autocovariance, 4
  choice of divisor in estimate, 9
  estimate of, 6
  function, 4
  generating function, 129
Autoregressive Moving Average process, 43–53

ARMA(1, 1), 45–51, 74
ARMA(p, q), 43–5
Autoregressive operator, 15, 99
  generalised, 99
  seasonal, 124
Autoregressive process, 15–30
  AR(1), 15–9, 27
  AR(2), 19–27, 30
  AR(p), 15, 26–30

Backcasting, 70
Backshift operator, 12
Bartlett, M. S., 6–7, 8, 12, 19, 175
Bartlett's formula, *see* Bartlett
Bates, J. M., 135, 177
Ben Nevis, *see* Series A and A*
Box, G. E. P., 14, 52, 68–9, 78, 82, 89, 129, 157, 175–6, 178
Box–Jenkins, 12–4, 157–8
Box–Pierce results, 78–84, 86
  for AR(1), 78–80
  for AR(2), 80–2
  for AR(p), 78–9
  for ARMA (p, q), 82–3
Brewer, K. R. W., 177
Buchan, A., 175

Chance significance, 18–9
Chatfield, C., 129, 135, 176
Coincidental case, 141, 150
Conditional expectation operator, 91
Continuous series, 1
Cooper, R. L., 176
Cost function, 135–6
Cox, D. R., 52, 178
Cross covariance, 43

Cumulative periodogram check, 86–9, 129

Department of Employment Gazette, 175
Deterministic series, 1
Deterministic trend, 111
Diagnostic checks, 75–89, 95
Dickinson, J. P., 135, 177
Difference equation form, 52
Difference operator, 12
  seasonal, 124
Differencing, 14, 99–117
  seasonal, 124–5, 128
Discrete series, 1
Dow Jones, *see* Series L
Duality between AR and MA, 42

E.f.f., *see* Eventual forecast function
Econometric models, 134–5
Ensemble, 1
  values, 4
Equivalence of AR and MA models, 32, 74
Ergodicity, 5
Estimation, 14, 68–74
Eventual forecast function, 97
  for ARMA(1, 2), 97–8
  for ARMA (p, q), 97
  for ARIMA(1, 1, 0), 117–8
  for ARIMA (p, d, q), 117, 122
  for IMA(1, 1), 119
  for IMA(2, 2), 117–8
EWMA, 120
Exponential smoothing, 123, 158
  formula, 119
Exponentially weighted moving average, 120
Explosive process, 53, 157

Financial Times, 175
Forecast error variance, 92
  for AR(1), 120
  for ARMA(1, 1), 120
  for IMA(1, 1), 121
  for non-stationary process, 120
Forecast errors, 90–1
  correlation between, 91–2
  expected values, 91
Forecast function, 90–1, 93
  see also Eventual forecast function
Forecasting, 90–8, 134–6
Forecasts,
  as diagnostic check, 95

combination of, 134–5
confidence limits, 93–4
effect of parameter estimation errors, 96–7
minimum mean square error, 90
minimum variance, 93
robustness of, 96–9
unbiased, 91
updating, 93–4
weights, 90, 135

Gaussian process, 3
Granger, C. W. J., 95, 135–42, 150–1, 175–8
Granger's Lemma, 138–41, 146
Grid-search, 69

Harrison, P. J., 158, 177
Holt, C. C., 158

ICI, *see* Series D and D*
ICL, 68, 133, 176
Identification, 14, 54–67
  program, 167–72
Initial estimates, 57–8
Integrated process, 99–123
International airline passengers, *see* Series M
Interpretation of models, 134–45, 151
Inverted form, 52
Invertibility, 31–2, 36
  for ARMA(1, 1), 44, 52
  for ARMA (p, q), 43
  for MA(1), 32
  for MA(2), 37
  for MA(1) × MA(1)$_{12}$, 128–9

Jenkins, G. M., 9, 14, 68–9, 89, 129, 157, 175, 178

Kolmogorov–Smirnov test, 87

Lag, 4
Lead, 90
Length of series, 1
  necessary, 6
  effective, 113, 129
Leuthold, R. M., 176
Level, 99, 120
Linear filter, 13

Mabert, V. A., 178
MacCormick, A. J. A., 176
Makridakis, S., 178
Main theorem, 139
Mann, H. B., 176

Marginal non-invertibility, 36, 154
Mean of process, 3−4
  estimate of, 6
Meteorology of Nottingham, 175
Microbe multiplying, 157
Mixed process, *see* Autoregressive
    Moving Average process
Model multiplicity, 36
Model of process, 12
  AR(1), 15
  AR(2), 19
  AR(p), 15
  ARMA(p, q), 43
  ARIMA(p, d, q), 99
  MA(1), 32
  MA(2), 37
  MA(q), 31
  Multiplicative, 124−5
  SARIMA, 124−5, 128
Monthly Digest of Statistics, 176
Moving Average inequalities, 56, 58,
    137
  proof, 173−4
Moving Average operator, 31
Moving Average process, 31−42
  MA(1), 32−36
  MA(2), 37−42
  MA(q), 31−2, 42
  necessary and sufficient condition,
    137−8
Moving sum, 153−4

Naylor, T. H., 177
Neave, H., 178
Newbold, P., 133, 135, 177−8
Non-stationarity, 3
  homogeneous, 99−103
Nottingham castle
  rainfall, *see* Series R
  temperature, *see* Series B and B*

Observation error model, 141
Observation interval, 1
Order in probability, 78
Overdifferencing, 102
Overfit, 75

P.a.c.f., *see* Partial autocorrelation
    function
Parameter estimates,
  initial values, 57
  redundancy, 70−1
  standard errors of, 70
  see also Estimation

Parsimony, 14
Partial autocorrelation, 9−10
  estimate of, 10
  standard error of, 10
Partial autocorrelation function, 9
  for AR(1), 11, 16−8
  for AR(2), 20−4
  for AR(p), 28
  for ARMA(1, 1), 45−51
  for ARMA(p, q), 44−5
  for MA(1), 33−6
  for MA(2), 38−51
  for white noise, 13
  relation with autoregressive
    parameters, 28
  sampling properties, 10
Parzen, E., 175
Passenger miles, *see* Series P
Period sum, 153−5
Periodogram, 87
Pierce, D. A., 78, 82, 176
Pivotal value, 97
Portmanteau test, 84
Process, 1
  control, 158
Prothero, D. L., 129, 135, 176
Pseudo-periodic behaviour, 25

Quenouille, M. H., 10, 175
Quenouille's formula, *see* Quenouille

Radcliffe, R. C., 178
Random shock form, 52
Random walk, 113
Realisability, 146−52
Reid, D. J., 6, 133, 175
Residuals, *see* Shock estimates

Sales of Company X, *see* Series Q
Samples series, 1
SARIMA, 124
Seasonal models, 124−33
Schmitz, A., 176
Seaks, T. G., 177
Series examples,
  A, 1−2
  A*, 114−6, 132−3, 159
  B, 1−2
  B*, 160
  C, 1−2
  D, 1−2, 7−8, 10−1
  D*, 102−3, 105−6, 116, 119, 121,
    129, 132, 160
  E, 1−2

Series examples (*contd.*)
E*, 126, 128–30, 132, 161
F, 1–4, 7–8, 11
F*, 121–2, 161
G, 7–8, 65–6, 72, 76, 83, 86, 88–9, 94–6, 107, 162
H, 65–6, 72–3, 162
J, 66–7, 163
K, 73, 88–9, 95–6, 132–3, 163
L, 107–8, 113, 132–3, 164
M, 124–6, 128–30, 132, 164
P, 126, 128–30, 132, 165
Q, 126, 128–9, 131–2, 157, 165
R, 126, 128–9, 131–2, 166
Shock estimates, 68, 77–8, 82
autocorrelations of, 78–84
modelling, 85–6
Shock sum of squares, 68
surface, 69
Shocks, 12
estimated, 68–9
Siegel, S., 176
Simple model, 74
Simulations,
AR(1), 16–7
AR(2), 20–3
ARMA(1, 1), 46–51
MA(1), 34–5
MA(2), 38–41
white noise, 13
Skipped series, 156
Slutsky, E., 154, 177
Slutsky effect *see* **Slutsky**
Space series, 157
Stable series, 103
Starting values, 69
Stationarity, 3–4
of order p, 3
strict, 3
weak, 3–4
Stationarity conditions,
for AR(1), 15
for AR(2), 24–5
for AR(p), 15, 28–9
for ARMA(1, 1), 44, 52
for ARMA (p, q), 43
Statistical process, 1
Statistical series, 1
Stochastic trend, 101
Substantial difference, 72
Sunspot numbers, *see* Series K

Thompson, H. E., 157, 176
Tiao, G. C., 155, 157, 176–7
Time series, 1
Time values, 4–5
Tintner, G., 176
Tomasek, O., 178
Traffic wardens, 145
Transfer function, 13
modelling, 158
Transformation of series, 45, 52, 136, 157
Trivedi, P. K., 176

Unstable series, 103

Variance of,
AR(1), 15
AR(2), 24
AR(p), 26
ARMA(1, 1), 45
MA(1), 32
MA(2), 37
MA(q), 31
Variance of differenced series, 110–2, 117
Variance of process, 4
estimate of, 6
Variance of series mean, 55
Variate Differencing, 116–7, 125, 128
Verification, 14, 75–89
Visual extrapolation, 95–6

Wald, A., 176
Waldmeier, M., 176
Watts, D. G., 9, 175–6
Weights of function, 13
Wheelwright, S., 178
White noise, 12–3
Whittle, P., 157, 177
Wichern, D. W., 176–7
Winters, P. R., 158, 176
Wölfer sunspots data, *see* Series K
Wold, H., 137–8, 177
Women unemployed, *see* Series E and E*
Wu, R. Y., 154, 177

Yule–Walker equations and estimates, 27